MAPPING

for CONGRESS

Supporting Public Policy with GIS

Library of Congress, Congressional Cartography Program

Edited by	Nancy Sappington
with	Christopher Thomas
	Milton Ospina
	Brent Roderick
	Ray Carnes
	Michael Law
	Polly Barbee
Designed by	Amaree Israngkura

ESRI wishes to thank the Congressional Cartography Program of the Geography and Map Division, Library of Congress, Ginny Mason and Jacob Zonn, for their contributions to this publication. The maps in chapter 2, Current Public Policy Projects, were designed by Ginny Mason, Cartographer.

ESRI, 380 New York Street, Redlands, California 92373-8100

Printed in the United States of America

Library of Congress Cataloging-in-Publication Data
Mapping for Congress : supporting public policy with GIS : Library of Congress, Congressional Cartography
Program / edited by Nancy Sappington ... [et al.] ; designed by Amaree Israngkura.
    p.   cm.
    ISBN 1-58948-145-3
    1. Geographic information systems—Government policy—United States. 2. Information storage and
retrieval systems—Geography—Government policy—United States. 3. Cartography—Government policy—
United States. 4. Information storage and retrieval systems—Cartography—Government policy—United States.
I. Sappington, Nancy, 1948– II. Congressional Cartography Program (Library of Congress)
G70.215.U6M25 2006
320.60285—dc22   2006000784

*This publication describes a current program at the Geography and Map Division of the Library of Congress. Please be advised that
the Library does not endorse a particular vendor, product, or service.*

Collecting and distributing information is fundamental to establishing good public policy at all levels of government in the United States. Whether it is for taxation, regulation, the funding of public programs, or providing services, accurate data is crucial.

GIS technology is providing access to our country's cultural and physical geographic knowledge. This is helping local, state, and federal agencies make better decisions and more effectively coordinate their efforts. Finally, GIS is helping governments at all levels connect with their citizens in a visual and analytical framework that is easy to understand.

The maps in the first part of this book highlight some of the outstanding work from the Library of Congress Geography and Map Division's Congressional Cartography Program. This program should be used as a model for starting similar GIS and mapping services throughout public organizations and government agencies. The maps exemplify the creativity of the Library of Congress GIS professionals and show how they use the technology to help members of Congress and congressional staff understand the context of change and what it means.

The maps in the last section of the book show how GIS can be used to provide insight into national trends and how these patterns might influence current and future public policy.

Warm regards,

Jack Dangermond
President, ESRI

Table of Contents

1

GIS—Helping to Formulate Public Policy

GIS—Helping to Formulate Public Policy

For the legislative process to work effectively, the U.S. Congress relies on a multidisciplined approach for authoritative, nonpartisan, timely, and objective analysis and research of issues to define policy problems, evaluate laws, and support implementation oversight. In the end, decisions represent a compromise that the majority of a constituency supports, or they are based on evidence that provides a foundation for taking a strong position.

The intention of this book is to promote the value of GIS technology and illustrate to elected officials and others involved in the legislative process how GIS can be a valuable tool in the public policy-making process.

Relevant, persuasive, irrefutable data can turn the tide in a debate about legislation. It is a key reason why elected officials invest in a cause. Government officials and their staff members are confronted daily with a multitude of issues. All issues are important, but some have to mark time as the most urgent on the agenda are dealt with first. Helping to efficiently manage problems in a timely manner has been the hallmark of GIS. It brings clarity to a range of subjects and stirs enthusiasm in those it touches. The case studies in this book show how GIS can save time in the discovery process while helping to substantiate a position.

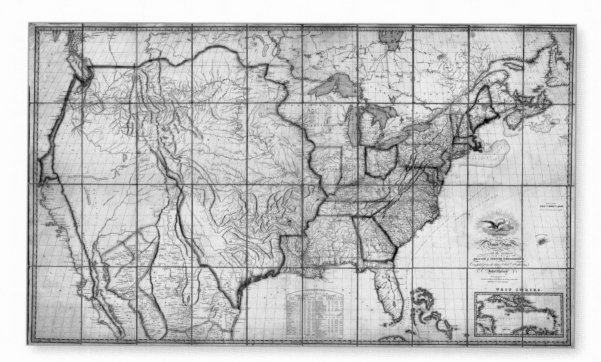

Early map production methods were time-consuming and laborious.

Map of the United States with the Contiguous British and Spanish Possessions (John Melish, 1816) Image courtesy of DavidRumsey.com

What Is a GIS?

As cartography has evolved, map production has moved from labor-intensive processes to automated methods. Technology has succeeded in making the world smaller while expanding each individual's world. One innovation that has drastically altered the nature of cartography is GIS technology, which emphasizes the use of spatial data in digital formats and provides a framework for the systematic measurement of geography. In addition to automating cartographic techniques, GIS enables sophisticated geographic analysis and can be integrated with other computer technologies such as satellite imagery for complex image analysis. Today, cartography and GIS are moving into an era of enterprise information technology that takes advantage of innovations in the storage, replication, and management of data.

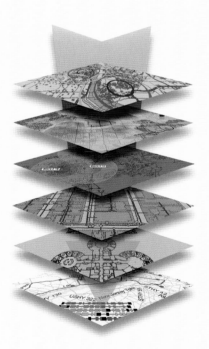

By connecting databases to maps, GIS helps make intricate and abstract problems real and concrete and helps elected officials manage their complexity more effectively. It combines layers of information about where things are with descriptive data about those things and their surroundings such as income levels, air quality, growth patterns, disease incidence, or voting trends. Information about where a point is located on a map, the distance from one point to another, or what is located within a specific area can be stored in digital format in layers or themes of the GIS. By combining a range of spatially referenced data and analytic tools, GIS technology enables government officials to prioritize issues, understand them, consider alternatives, and reach viable conclusions. The ability of a GIS to link datasets together by common location information facilitates the sharing of information whether it is interdepartmentally within an organization or via the Internet with the public.

Government Is about Geography

Among the greatest challenges that decision makers face is the realization that every decision affects something else and knowing what those effects can be.

Establishing public policy—whether it is in the realm of health and human services, economic development, transportation, environmental stewardship, criminal justice, education, public infrastructure, or public safety—can often be a complicated process in which diverse opinions clash, and the consequences of certain policies are sometimes not fully realized. In a world where information abounds, the art of developing effective public policy has become more challenging as policy makers try to assimilate an endless stream of facts.

Governing and the subsequent enactment of public policy have taken broad turns throughout history. In general, the populace looks to its civic leaders to provide for their safety, health, and welfare. Embracing these ideals has led policy makers and elected officials to seek experts in a range of fields including science, agriculture, health care, education, social science, and criminology. When specialists from different areas of expertise come to the table with varying assessments and opinions, a GIS can help bring issues into focus by integrating information from these disparate sources, making it easy to recognize changing situations and improving efficiency by visualizing the long-term effects of actions.

GIS in the Policy-Making Life Cycle

It is no secret that nearly everything that occurs in public policy making happens in the context of geography. Maps have always been a part of the governing process. Knowing the *where* is paramount to the other considerations of accountability. With this realization, GIS technology is becoming an integral part of the decision-making process as it helps to shape and influence choices.

2

Current Public Policy Projects

Current Public Policy Projects—The Magic of Maps

For centuries, humans have had a fascination with maps. Perhaps this is because we possess a remarkable ability to recognize and understand the environment and quickly derive large amounts of information from spatial images. Maps, which depict spatial images, have developed as a visual language revealing a treasure trove of secrets to those who look. In addition to helping us experience the world in which we live, maps have enabled us to travel through time. We can retrace our ancestors' footsteps, locate where we are, or plan a future adventure.

The tools for applying this sense of place to human issues have been developing for centuries. Relying on human creativity and expression, cartographers have used a range of techniques to represent the world we live in. Historically, maps have been produced for specific purposes such as to show jurisdictional boundaries, highlight landscape features, or illustrate themes such as population and other demographic information.

The Library of Congress, the largest library in the world, began collecting maps and atlases when it purchased three maps and an atlas from a London dealer in the 1800s. Today, the library's cartographic holdings have grown to more than five million, dating from the fourteenth century and covering any subject and every country. In addition to maps and atlases, its collections include globes, models, remotely sensed images, and digital files.

While the Library of Congress functions as an information repository for Congress, this cache attracts researchers and scholars from around the world. Serving as the National Map Library, the Library of Congress Geography and Map Division oversees the greater part of these holdings, many of which are unique, and facilitates their use for those seeking information.

GIS and the Library of Congress

The Congressional Cartography Program (CCP) was established in 2003 to provide cartographic products and GIS services to Congress and the Congressional Research Service, the public policy research branch that provides objective analysis and research on all legislative issues to Congress. Housed in the Library of Congress Geography and Map Division, CCP is a one-stop GIS shop where congressional personnel can obtain geographic information and services to assist in making better-informed public policy decisions.

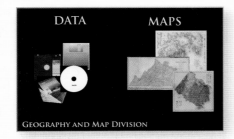

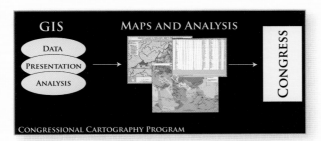

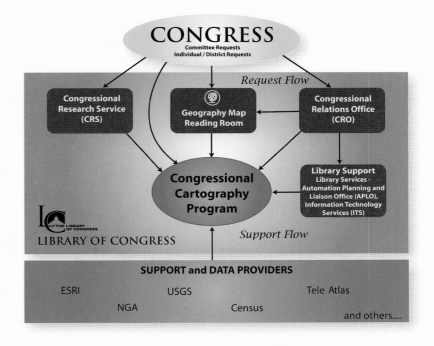

While CCP helps keep the Geography and Map Division's collections current and useful to the library's users and assists in documenting the historical development and use of GIS, it is focused on acquiring data, integrating it, and developing customized cartographic design applications for Congress and the Congressional Research Service.

To serve Congress in a timely manner, CCP has developed a map template approach to cartographic production that enables efficient creation of frequently requested core products such as maps of congressional districts, individual states, countries, U.S. ZIP Codes, and thematic distributions of various data on a national scale. This frees up staff time for more complex analysis and developing other services such as implementing design standards and other templates for more predictive maps that can answer questions such as "what's happening in my district?" For its central database, CCP has compiled data from various U.S. agencies and information from its own ongoing projects.

While still in its early stages of development, CCP has already begun to receive sophisticated GIS requests, and CCP staff members have developed close relationships with congressional staff as they provide the tools to investigate each issue while promoting the value of GIS. The following maps are some examples of the best work from CCP.

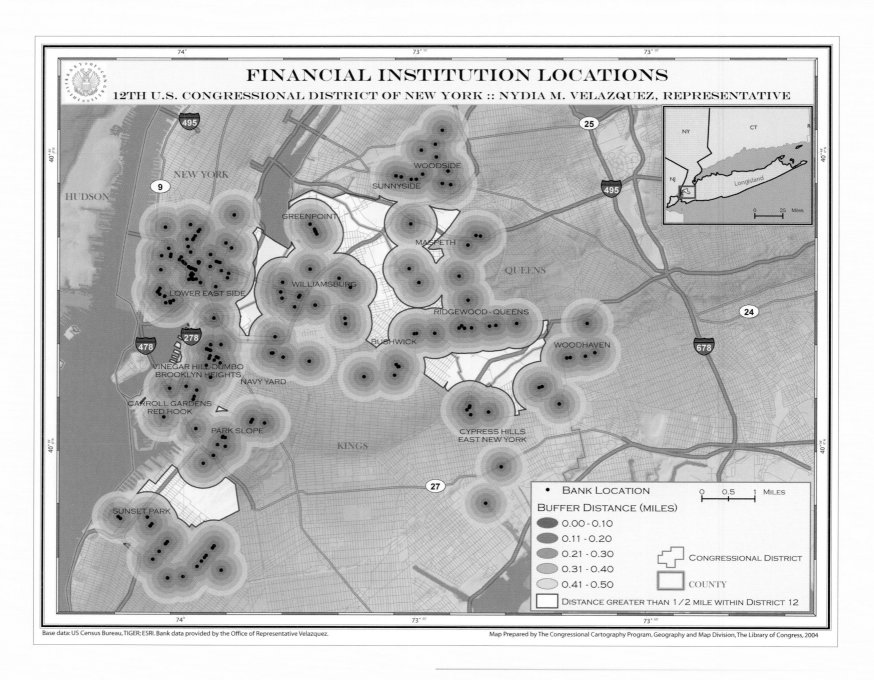

FINANCIAL INSTITUTION LOCATIONS

12TH U.S. CONGRESSIONAL DISTRICT OF NEW YORK :: NYDIA M. VELAZQUEZ, REPRESENTATIVE

• BANK LOCATION

BUFFER DISTANCE (MILES)
0.00 - 0.10
0.11 - 0.20
0.21 - 0.30
0.31 - 0.40
0.41 - 0.50

CONGRESSIONAL DISTRICT

COUNTY

DISTANCE GREATER THAN 1/2 MILE WITHIN DISTRICT 12

Base data: US Census Bureau, TIGER; ESRI. Bank data provided by the Office of Representative Velazquez.

Map Prepared by The Congressional Cartography Program, Geography and Map Division, The Library of Congress, 2004

Financial Institution Locations

This map shows areas within the 12th Congressional District in New York City that are underserved by financial institutions. The white areas that fall outside of the green buffer circles are more than one-half mile from a bank and are considered underserved.

Representative Nydia M. Velazquez (New York 12)

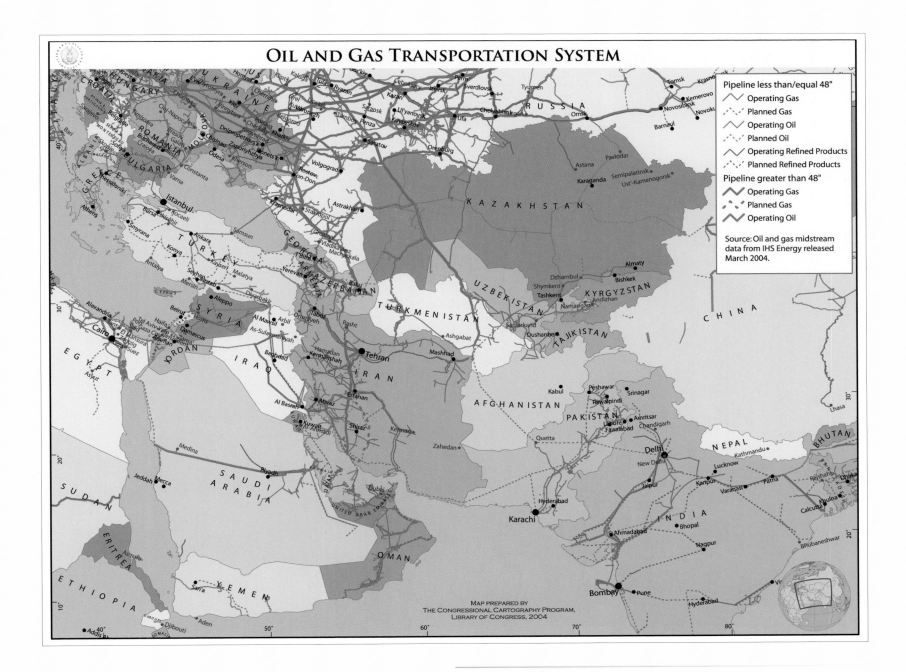

Oil and Gas Transportation System

This map depicts operating and planned oil and gas pipelines in the Middle East. It was produced from data compiled by IHS Energy, a major provider of data to energy companies, as of March 2004.

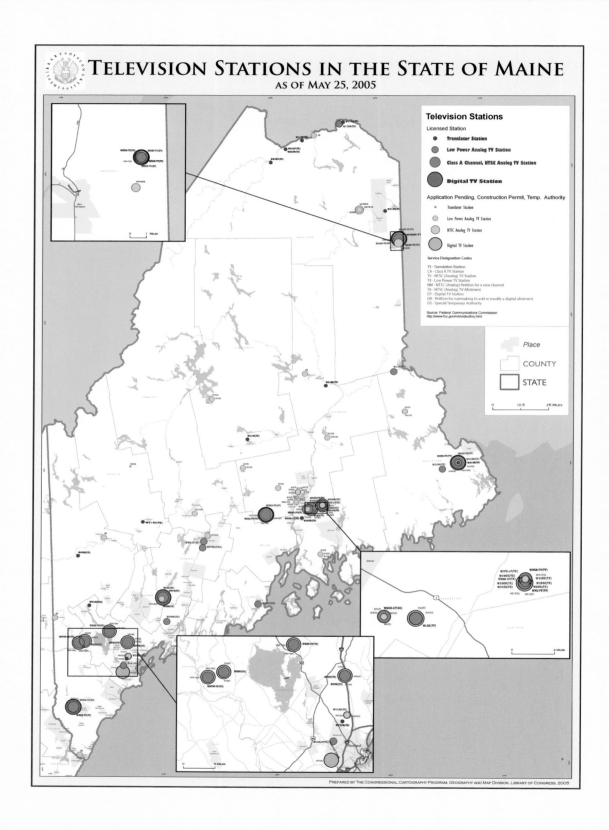

Television Stations in the State of Maine

The Congressional Cartography Program created this map for Senator Olympia J. Snowe (Maine) while the U.S. Congress (House and Senate) was considering legislation known as the Digital Television Transition Act of 2005. The purpose of the bill is to set a date when broadcasters must return their analog spectrum to the government. Broadcasters currently hold the digital and analog spectrum. The transition may disrupt service to some rural areas, especially those that receive signals from translators. This map was created to help Senator Snowe make policy decisions to ensure minimal consumer disruption.

Senator Olympia Snowe (Maine)

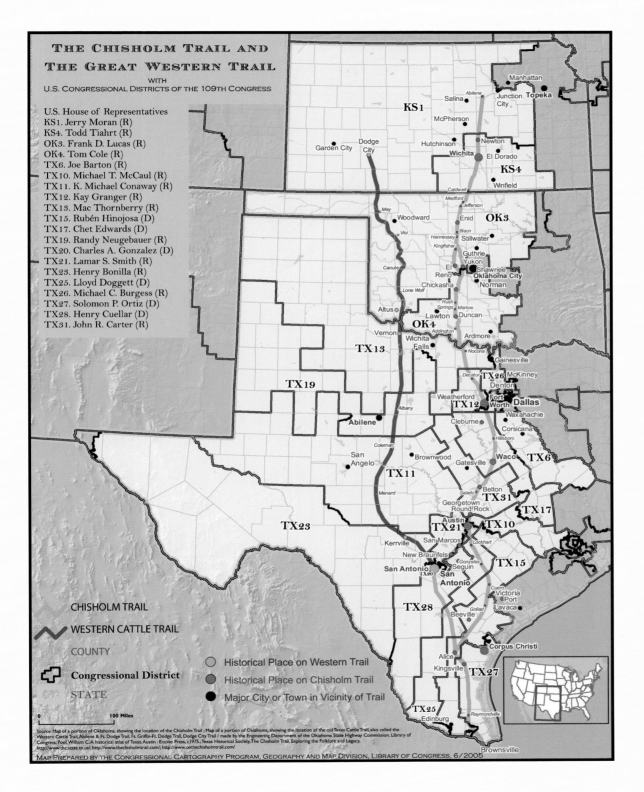

THE CHISHOLM TRAIL AND
THE GREAT WESTERN TRAIL
WITH
U.S. CONGRESSIONAL DISTRICTS OF THE 109TH CONGRESS

U.S. House of Representatives
KS1. Jerry Moran (R)
KS4. Todd Tiahrt (R)
OK3. Frank D. Lucas (R)
OK4. Tom Cole (R)
TX6. Joe Barton (R)
TX10. Michael T. McCaul (R)
TX11. K. Michael Conaway (R)
TX12. Kay Granger (R)
TX13. Mac Thornberry (R)
TX15. Rubén Hinojosa (D)
TX17. Chet Edwards (D)
TX19. Randy Neugebauer (R)
TX20. Charles A. Gonzalez (D)
TX21. Lamar S. Smith (R)
TX23. Henry Bonilla (R)
TX25. Lloyd Doggett (D)
TX26. Michael C. Burgess (R)
TX27. Solomon P. Ortiz (D)
TX28. Henry Cuellar (D)
TX31. John R. Carter (R)

CHISHOLM TRAIL
WESTERN CATTLE TRAIL
COUNTY
Congressional District
STATE

⊙ Historical Place on Western Trail
⦿ Historical Place on Chisholm Trail
⚫ Major City or Town in Vicinity of Trail

0   100 Miles

Source: Map of a portion of Oklahoma, showing the location of the Chisholm Trail ; Map of a portion of Oklahoma, showing the location of the old Texas Cattle Trail, also called the Western Cattle Trail, Abilene & Ft. Dodge Trail, Ft. Griffin-Ft. Dodge Trail, Dodge City Trail / made by the Engineering Department of the Oklahoma State Highway Commission. Library of Congress; Pool, William C. A historical atlas of Texas. Austin : Encino Press, c1975.; Texas Historical Society, The Chisholm Trail, Exploring the Folklore and Legacy,
http://www.thc.state.tx.us/; http://www.thechisholmtrail.com/; http://www.onthechisholmtrail.com/

MAP PREPARED BY THE CONGRESSIONAL CARTOGRAPHY PROGRAM, GEOGRAPHY AND MAP DIVISION, LIBRARY OF CONGRESS, 6/2005

The Chisholm Trail and the Great Western Trail

This map was produced in preparation for the introduction of a bill to the U.S. House of Representatives that proposed to amend the National Trails System Act. The amendment would designate the Chisholm Trail and Great Western Trail historic cattle drive trails for study and for potential addition to the National Trails System.

Representative Tom Cole (Oklahoma 4)

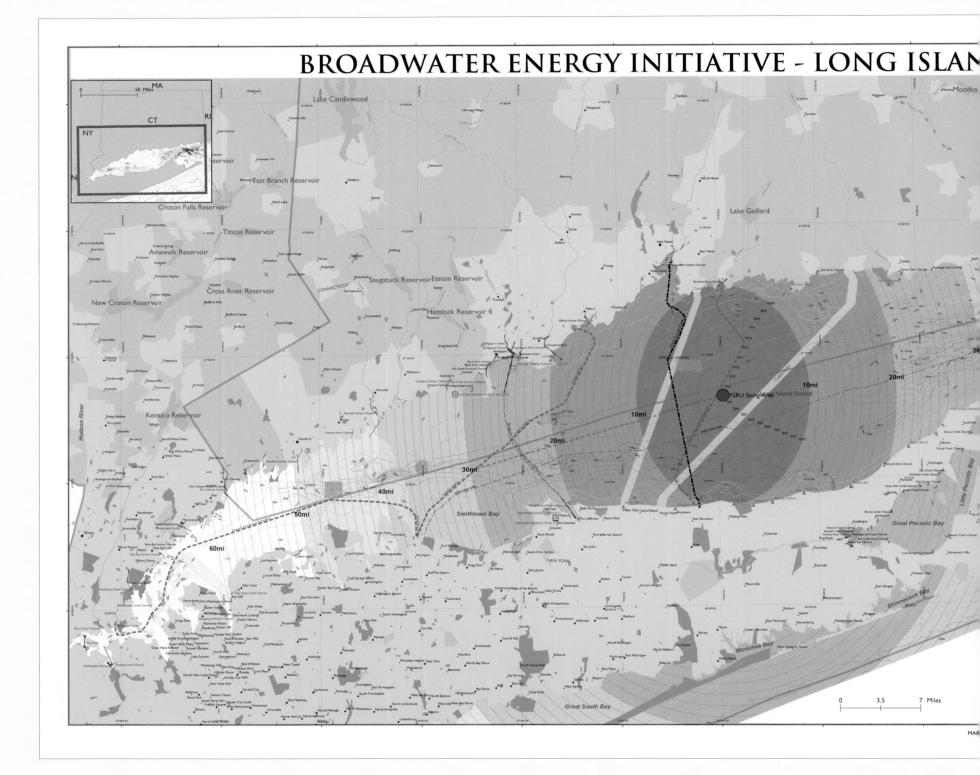

BROADWATER ENERGY INITIATIVE - LONG ISLAN

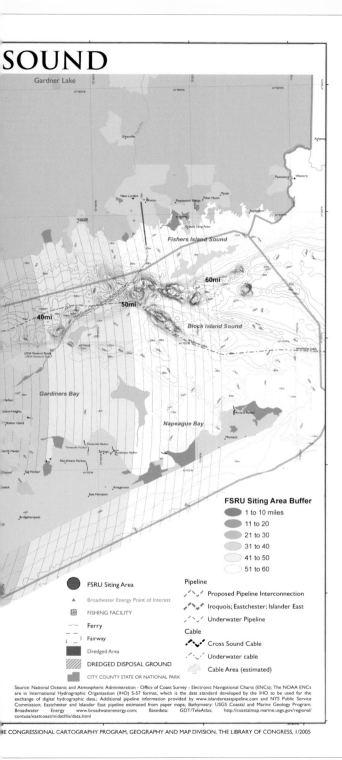

SOUND

FSRU Siting Area Buffer
- 1 to 10 miles
- 11 to 20
- 21 to 30
- 31 to 40
- 41 to 50
- 51 to 60

⬤ FSRU Siting Area
▲ Broadwater Energy Point of Interest
🏢 FISHING FACILITY
⌁ Ferry
⌁ Fairway
▦ Dredged Area
▨ DREDGED DISPOSAL GROUND
CITY COUNTY STATE OR NATIONAL PARK

Pipeline
Proposed Pipeline Interconnection
Iroquois; Eastchester; Islander East
Underwater Pipeline

Cable
Cross Sound Cable
Underwater cable
Cable Area (estimated)

Source: National Oceanic and Atmospheric Administration - Office of Coast Survey - Electronic Navigational Charts (ENCs); The NOAA ENCs are in International Hydrographic Organization (IHO) S-57 format, which is the data standard developed by the IHO to be used for the exchange of digital hydrographic data.; Additional pipeline information provided by the.islandereastpipeline.com and NYS Public Service Commission; Eastchester and Islander East pipeline estimated from paper maps; Bathymetry: USGS Coastal and Marine Geology Program; Broadwater Energy www.broadwaterenergy.com; Basedata: GDT/TeleAtlas; http://coastalmap.marine.usgs.gov/regional/contusa/eastcoast/midatl/lis/data.html

THE CONGRESSIONAL CARTOGRAPHY PROGRAM, GEOGRAPHY AND MAP DIVISION, THE LIBRARY OF CONGRESS, 1/2005

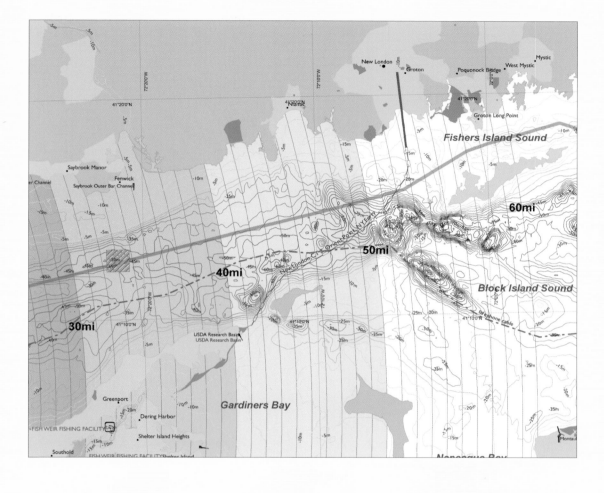

Broadwater Energy Initiative—Long Island Sound

This map was created to help visualize the possible impacts of a liquefied natural gas (LNG) facility that had been proposed for Long Island Sound. Issues such as the exact location of the facility and size of potential exclusion zones around it had not been resolved. The map provided a means for examining the facility's proximity to fishing grounds, pipelines, cable crossings, and other sensitive areas based on size and location.

The project Web site at www.broadwaterenergy.com covers in detail the implementation of the LNG project. In addition to preparing the map, the Congressional Cartography Program provided Senator Joe Lieberman's staff members with an ArcGIS® Publisher/ArcReader™ file to enable them to interact with the map.

Senator Joe Lieberman (Connecticut)

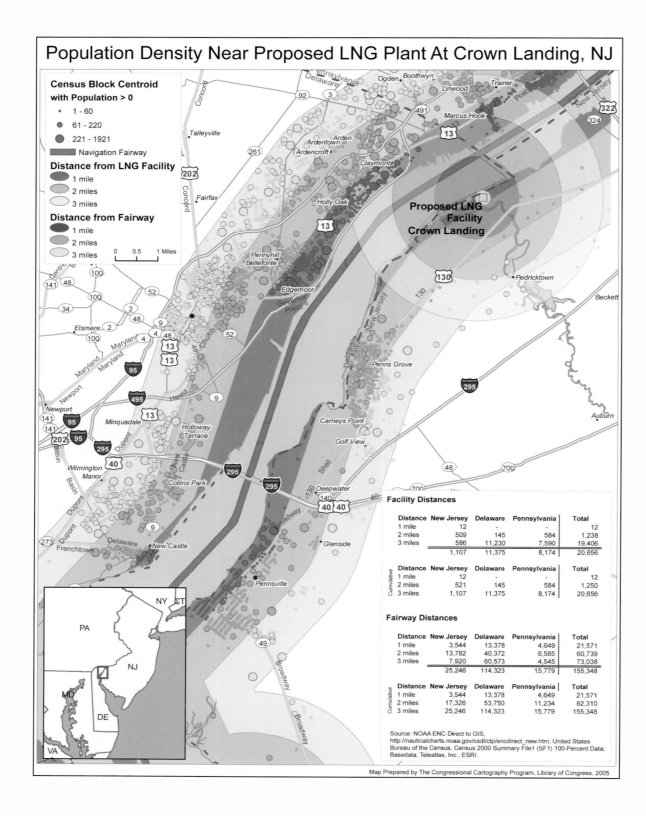

Population Density Near Proposed LNG Plant At Crown Landing, NJ

Census Block Centroid
with Population > 0
- 1 - 60
- 61 - 220
- 221 - 1921

Navigation Fairway

Distance from LNG Facility
- 1 mile
- 2 miles
- 3 miles

Distance from Fairway
- 1 mile
- 2 miles
- 3 miles

0   0.5   1 Miles

Facility Distances

Distance	New Jersey	Delaware	Pennsylvania	Total
1 mile	12	-	-	12
2 miles	509	145	584	1,238
3 miles	586	11,230	7,590	19,406
	1,107	11,375	8,174	20,656

Distance	New Jersey	Delaware	Pennsylvania	Total
1 mile	12	-	-	12
2 miles	521	145	584	1,250
3 miles	1,107	11,375	8,174	20,656

(Cumulative)

Fairway Distances

Distance	New Jersey	Delaware	Pennsylvania	Total
1 mile	3,544	13,378	4,649	21,571
2 miles	13,782	40,372	6,585	60,739
3 miles	7,920	60,573	4,545	73,038
	25,246	114,323	15,779	155,348

Distance	New Jersey	Delaware	Pennsylvania	Total
1 mile	3,544	13,378	4,649	21,571
2 miles	17,326	53,750	11,234	82,310
3 miles	25,246	114,323	15,779	155,348

(Cumulative)

Source: NOAA ENC Direct to GIS,
http://nauticalcharts.noaa.gov/csdl/ctp/encdirect_new.htm; United States
Bureau of the Census, Census 2000 Summary File1 (SF1) 100-Percent Data;
Basedata, Teleatlas, Inc.; ESRI.

Map Prepared by The Congressional Cartography Program, Library of Congress, 2005

Population Density Near Proposed LNG Plant at Crown Landing, NJ

This map was requested to determine potential hazard zones regarding a proposed liquefied natural gas (LNG) facility. Under the proposed plan, tankers carrying natural gas (refrigerated into a liquid state) would travel up the Delaware River and offload the fuel at a pier and storage facility in New Jersey. There are concerns that a terrorist attack or accident on the ship or storage facility could ignite the gas and cause a fire.

Using results from scientific studies and engineering codes, hazard zones can be calculated around the ship (according to its movement) and the storage facility. The map was requested to plot these zones, overlapped with the population density of the area. The resulting maps show how many people might be affected if a fire broke out on the tanker or at the storage facility.

Representative Robert Andrews (New Jersey 1)

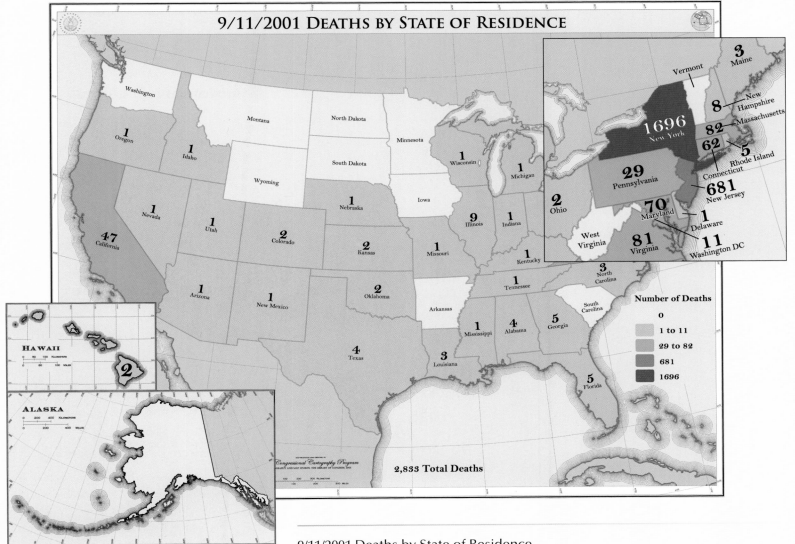

9/11/2001 DEATHS BY STATE OF RESIDENCE

2,833 Total Deaths

9/11/2001 Deaths by State of Residence

This map was used during testimony before the House Subcommittee on Immigration, Border Security, and Claims of the House Judiciary Committee in March 2005. While the U.S. Congress (House and Senate) was recommending the hiring of more special agents, the concern was that this would not be a sufficient number. This map was prepared to show Americans and U.S. representatives from various parts of the United States how their regions were affected by the attacks that took place in New York, Washington, and Pennsylvania and how the nation as a whole was vulnerable.

A map of the United States showing the number of casualties from each state helped provide a graphic illustration of how many people throughout the country were killed in the attacks. A revision of this map was also used in May 2005 during testimony before the same subcommittee about the new dual missions of the immigration enforcement agencies.

Majority Counsel, U.S. House of Representatives, Committee on the Judiciary

Persons Affected by Hurricane Katrina

These maps are the product of a larger project to investigate the demographic breakdown of persons affected by Hurricane Katrina. The Congressional Cartography Program did an analysis of population at the block level using Census 2000 data to determine a breakdown of the population living in the different categories of Federal Emergency Management Agency (FEMA)-assessed damage. The study is based on FEMA damage data as of September 21, 2005.

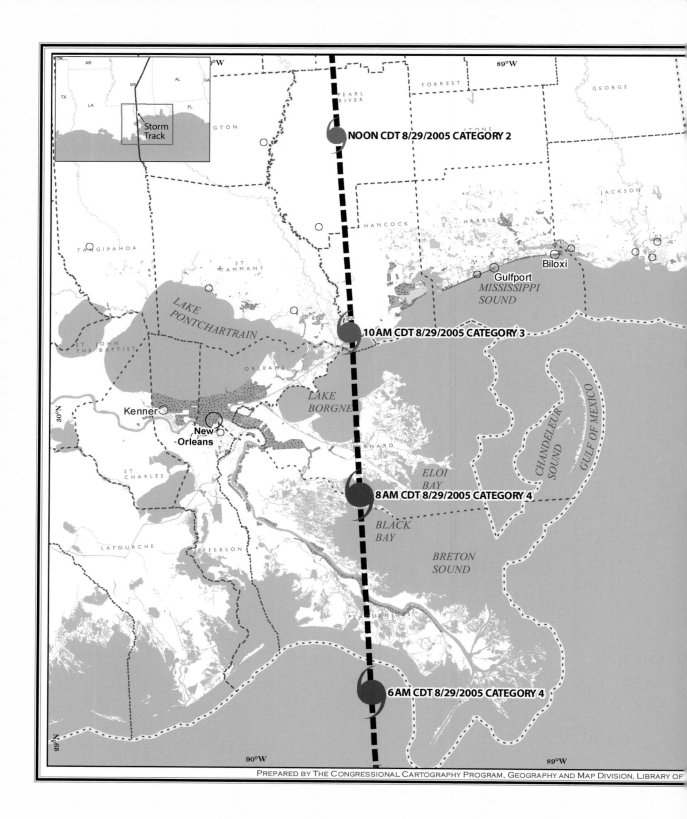

PREPARED BY THE CONGRESSIONAL CARTOGRAPHY PROGRAM, GEOGRAPHY AND MAP DIVISION, LIBRARY OF

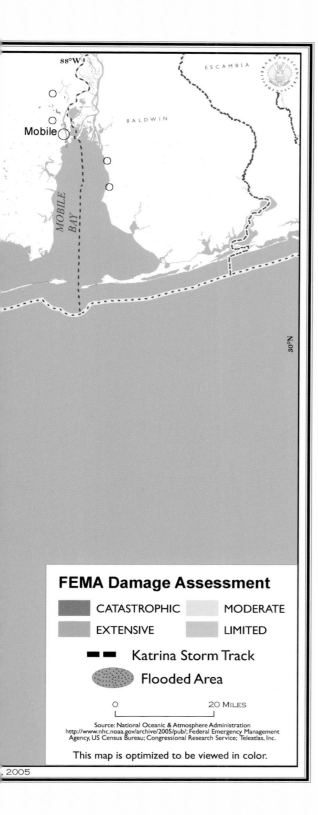

FEMA Damage Assessment

- CATASTROPHIC
- MODERATE
- EXTENSIVE
- LIMITED

▬ ▬ Katrina Storm Track

Flooded Area

0   20 MILES

Source: National Oceanic & Atmosphere Administration
http://www.nhc.noaa.gov/archive/2005/pub/; Federal Emergency Management
Agency, US Census Bureau; Congressional Research Service; Teleatlas, Inc.

This map is optimized to be viewed in color.

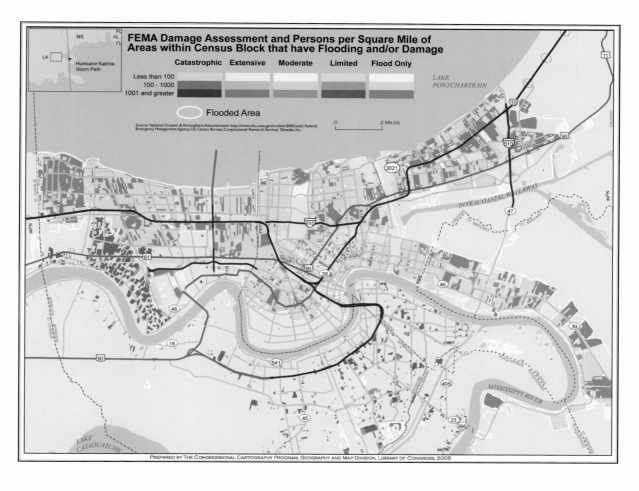

FEMA Damage Assessment and Persons per Square Mile of Areas within Census Block that have Flooding and/or Damage

	Catastrophic	Extensive	Moderate	Limited	Flood Only
Less than 100					
100 - 1000					
1001 and greater					

Flooded Area

Hurricane Katrina Storm Path

0   2 MILES

Source: National Oceanic & Atmosphere Administration http://www.nhc.noaa.gov/archive/2005/pub/; Federal Emergency Management Agency; US Census Bureau; Congressional Research Service; Teleatlas, Inc.

PREPARED BY THE CONGRESSIONAL CARTOGRAPHY PROGRAM, GEOGRAPHY AND MAP DIVISION, LIBRARY OF CONGRESS, 2005

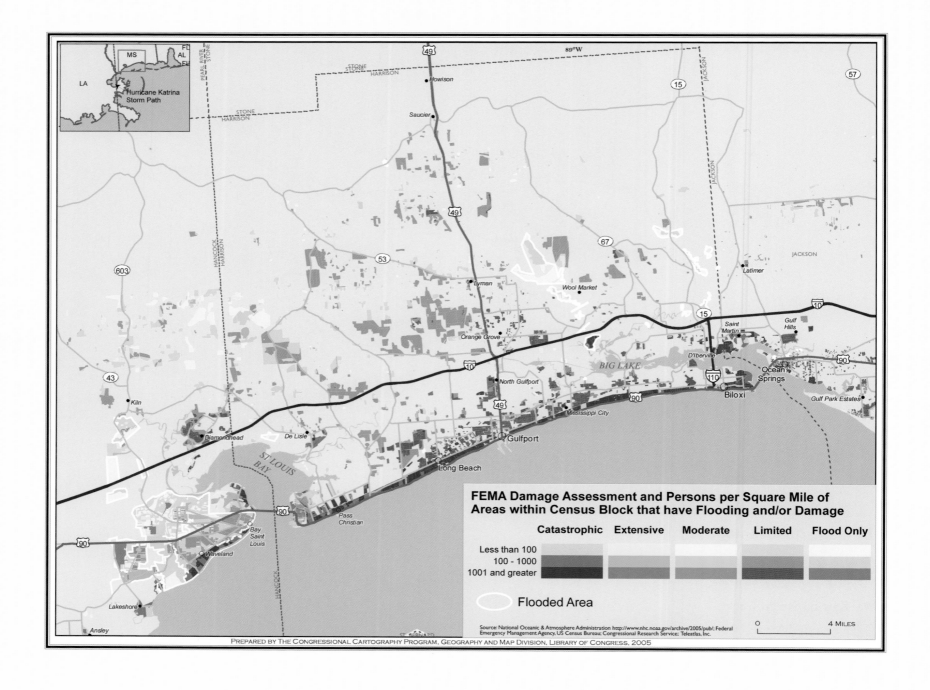

FEMA Damage Assessment and Persons per Square Mile of Areas within Census Block that have Flooding and/or Damage

	Catastrophic	Extensive	Moderate	Limited	Flood Only
Less than 100					
100 - 1000					
1001 and greater					

Flooded Area

Source: National Oceanic & Atmosphere Administration http://www.nhc.noaa.gov/archive/2005/pub/; Federal Emergency Management Agency, US Census Bureau; Congressional Research Service; Teleatlas, Inc.

0   4 MILES

PREPARED BY THE CONGRESSIONAL CARTOGRAPHY PROGRAM, GEOGRAPHY AND MAP DIVISION, LIBRARY OF CONGRESS, 2005

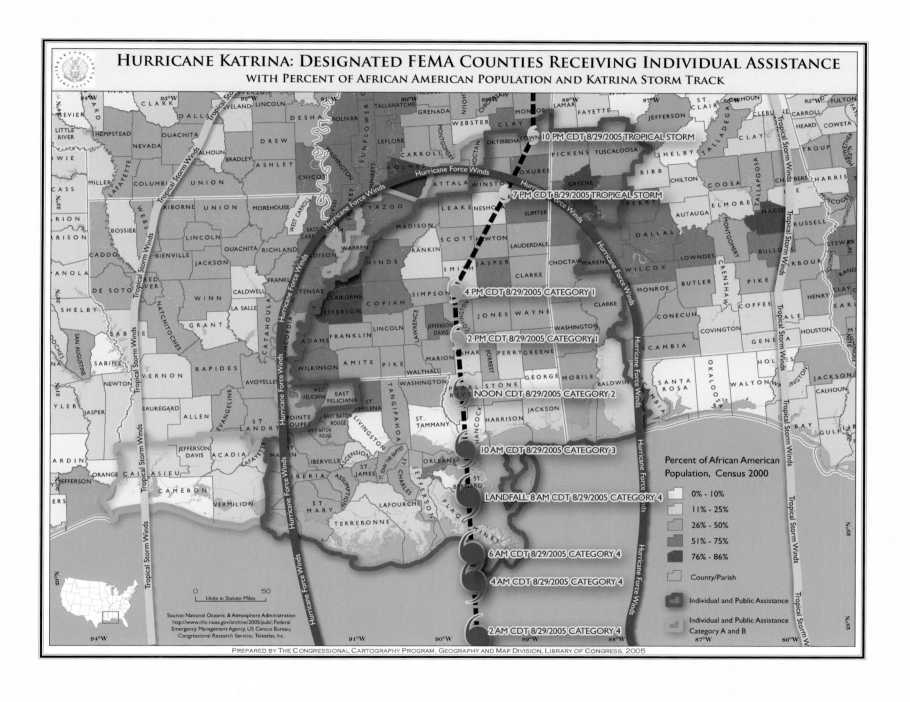

Hurricane Katrina: Designated FEMA Counties Receiving Individual Assistance
with Percent of African American Population and Katrina Storm Track

Source: National Oceanic & Atmosphere Administration
http://www.nhc.noaa.gov/archive/2005/pub/; Federal
Emergency Management Agency, US Census Bureau;
Congressional Research Service; Teleatlas, Inc.

Prepared by The Congressional Cartography Program, Geography and Map Division, Library of Congress, 2005

Percent of African American Population, Census 2000

0% - 10%
11% - 25%
26% - 50%
51% - 75%
76% - 86%
County/Parish
Individual and Public Assistance
Individual and Public Assistance Category A and B

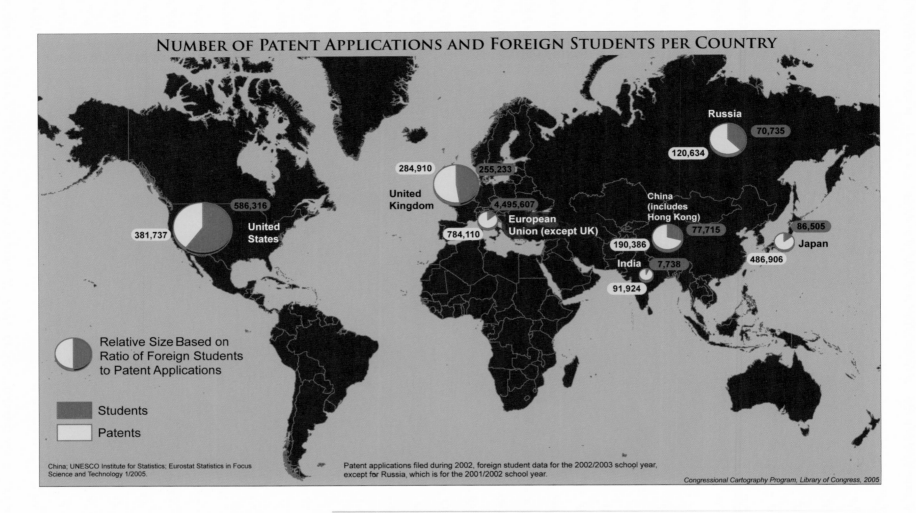

NUMBER OF PATENT APPLICATIONS AND FOREIGN STUDENTS PER COUNTRY

Russia
70,735
120,634

284,910
255,233
United Kingdom
4,495,607

586,316
United States
381,737

European Union (except UK)
784,110

China (includes Hong Kong)
77,715
190,386

86,505
Japan
486,906

India
7,738
91,924

Relative Size Based on Ratio of Foreign Students to Patent Applications

Students
Patents

China; UNESCO Institute for Statistics; Eurostat Statistics in Focus Science and Technology 1/2005.

Patent applications filed during 2002, foreign student data for the 2002/2003 school year, except for Russia, which is for the 2001/2002 school year.

Congressional Cartography Program, Library of Congress, 2005

Number of Patent Applications and Foreign Students per Country

This map was used during subcommittee hearings about economic and military espionage by foreign nationals in the United States.

Majority Counsel, U.S. House of Representatives, Committee on the Judiciary

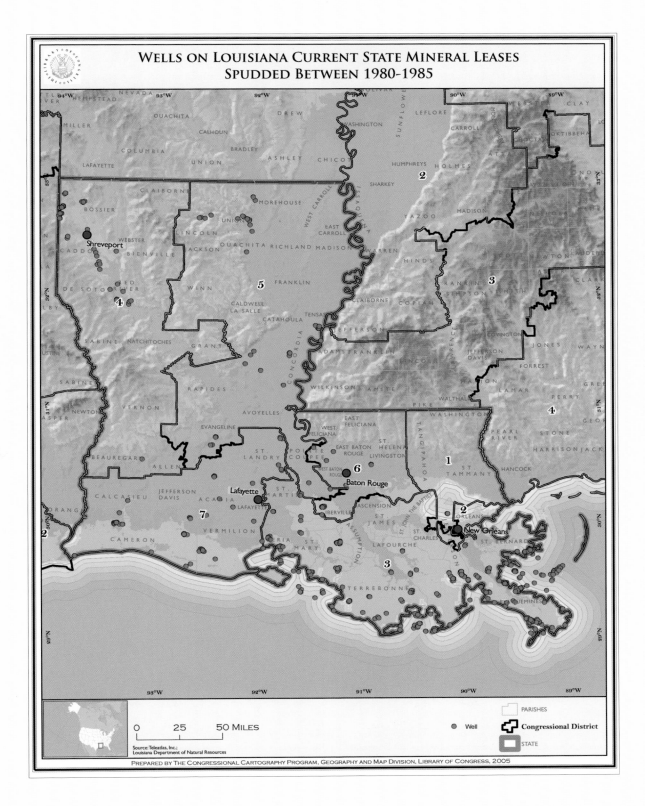

WELLS ON LOUISIANA CURRENT STATE MINERAL LEASES
SPUDDED BETWEEN 1980-1985

Wells on Louisiana Current State Mineral Leases Spudded between 1980 and 1985

This map was prepared before Hurricane Katrina to examine oil well locations in the state of Louisiana that were drilled between twenty and twenty-five years ago and that sit on current state-owned land or water. The data for this project was generated by the Louisiana Department of Natural Resources.

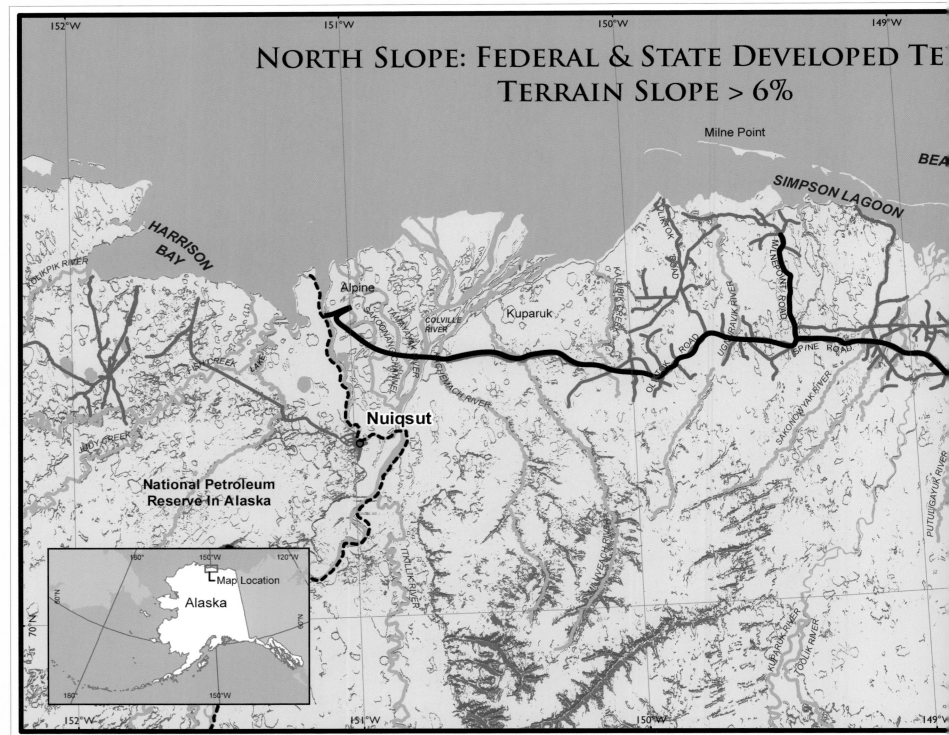

NORTH SLOPE: FEDERAL & STATE DEVELOPED TE
TERRAIN SLOPE > 6%

Source: National Elevation Dataset 30 meter/1 arc sec grid spacing resolution; National Atlas federal lands data;
Roads: Tele Atlas, Inc., Alaska Department of Natural Resources, and adapted from GAO and British Petroleum maps;
Universal Transverse Mercator Zone 5N NAD 83.

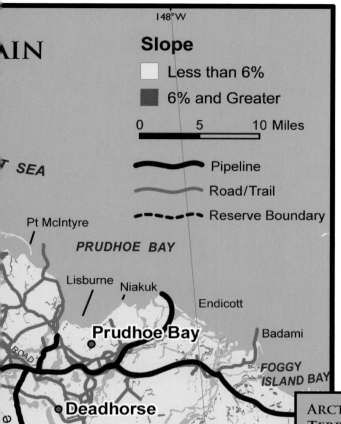

Slope

Less than 6%

6% and Greater

0   5   10 Miles

━━━ Pipeline

━━━ Road/Trail

- - - - Reserve Boundary

Pt McIntyre

PRUDHOE BAY

Lisburne   Niakuk

Endicott

Prudhoe Bay

Badami

*FOGGY
ISLAND BAY*

Deadhorse

Arctic National Wildlife Refuge Slope Maps

On Alaska's North Slope, exploration for oil and gas takes place in the wintertime. To decrease environmental impact, roads and drill pads are made of ice. If neither oil nor gas can be exploited immediately, exploration ceases, and the ice melts with little impact. This can significantly mitigate environmental damage in the exploration phase.

The area in and around Prudhoe Bay, developed using these techniques, is relatively flat. In the area that is proposed for development in the controversial Arctic Refuge, the terrain is mostly gently rolling. According to industry standards, the ice roads and ice pads cannot be built in terrain where the slope exceeds 6 percent.

These slope maps help answer questions about whether the environmental mitigation techniques are applicable in the area proposed for development in the refuge. The Marsh Creek Anticline is considered a promising area for oil and gas, but the maps show that a large portion of it is at a slope that would be somewhat prohibitive. Skirting the steeper areas with an ice road would result in a road that could be five times longer than one going straight across. These maps are a cartographic way of showing more clearly that lessons learned in already-developed areas might not always apply.

Representative Edward Markey (Massachusetts 7)

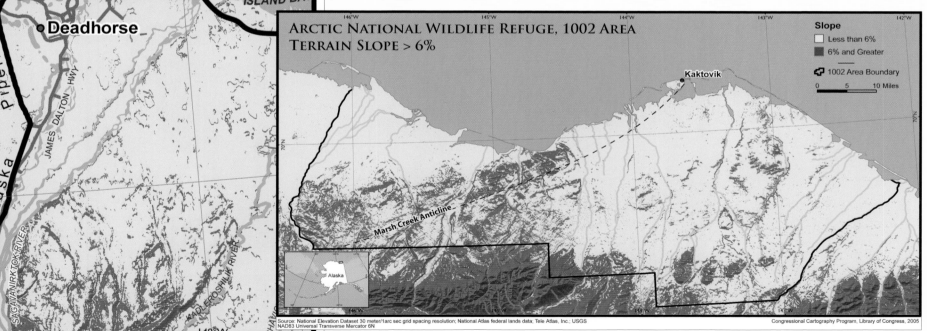

ARCTIC NATIONAL WILDLIFE REFUGE, 1002 AREA
TERRAIN SLOPE > 6%

Slope

Less than 6%

6% and Greater

1002 Area Boundary

0   5   10 Miles

Kaktovik

Marsh Creek Anticline

Alaska

Source: National Elevation Dataset 30 meter/1arc sec grid spacing resolution; National Atlas federal lands data; Tele Atlas, Inc.; USGS
NAD83 Universal Transverse Mercator 6N

Congressional Cartography Program, Library of Congress, 2005

Regional Jurisdictions

Several maps were created for this project, which was requested by Congressman Sam Farr. The composite map shows the discrete areas covered by eleven environmental agencies.

The United States divides environmental and natural resource protection among a variety of federal agencies. These agencies' regional organization does not reflect current understanding of ecosystems and connections between land, air, and water. After reading the Preliminary Report of the U.S. Commission on Ocean Policy (www.oceancommission.gov), Congressman Farr became interested in analyzing and actively considering how to restructure these regional offices to achieve a more unified system to oversee our environment and natural resources.

The maps provided by the Congressional Cartography Program at the Library of Congress were invaluable in visualizing how little geographical overlap exists between agencies. The maps continued to be useful as Congressman Farr had ongoing discussions on how to foster better communication between agencies and enable increased stewardship of all aspects of the environment from the land to the sea.

Representative Sam Farr (California 17)

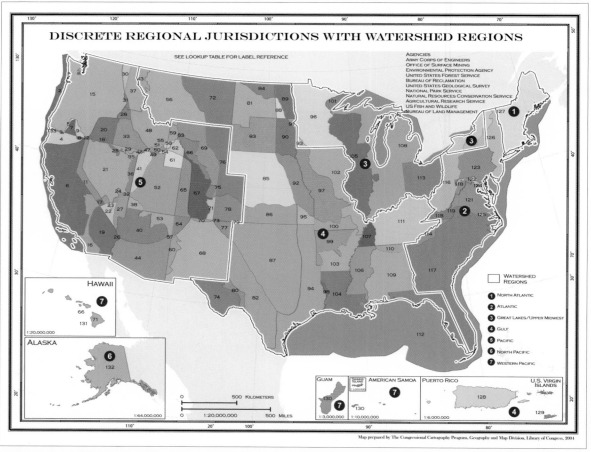

Composite map showing discrete areas covered by eleven environmental agencies

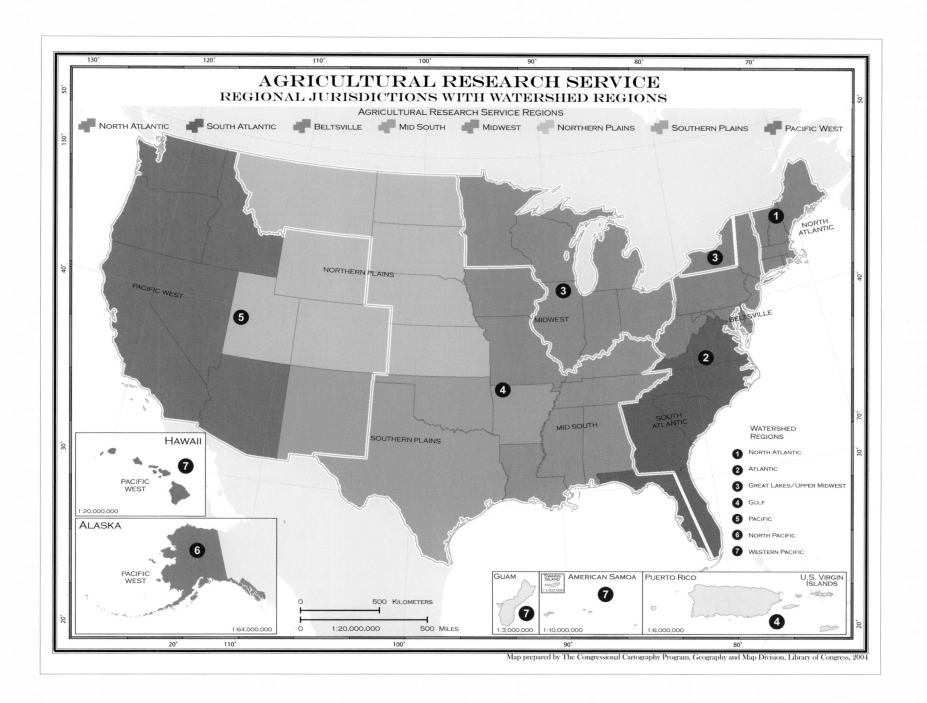

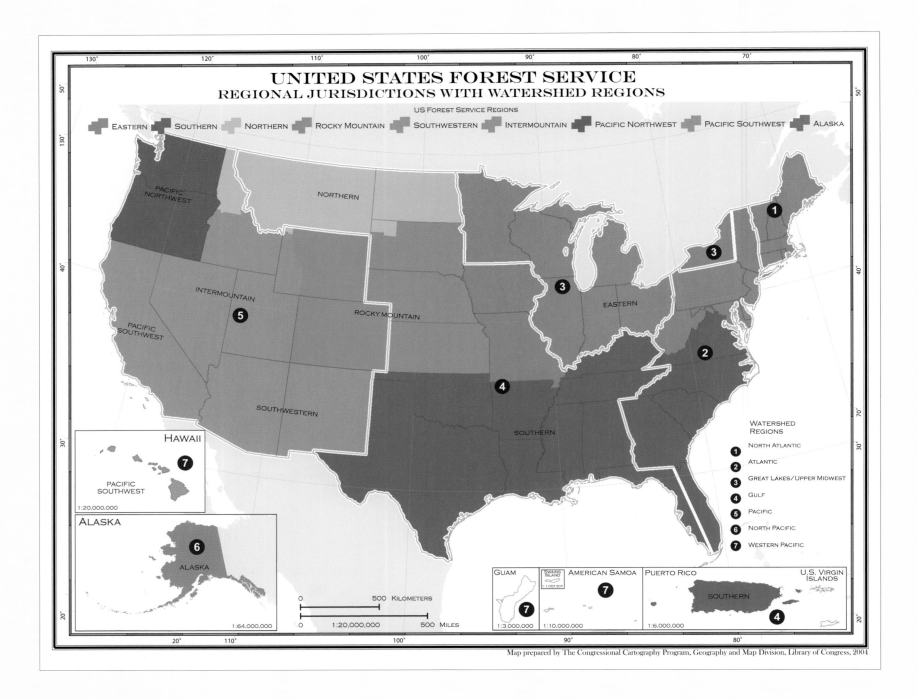

UNITED STATES FOREST SERVICE
REGIONAL JURISDICTIONS WITH WATERSHED REGIONS

US FOREST SERVICE REGIONS

EASTERN · SOUTHERN · NORTHERN · ROCKY MOUNTAIN · SOUTHWESTERN · INTERMOUNTAIN · PACIFIC NORTHWEST · PACIFIC SOUTHWEST · ALASKA

WATERSHED REGIONS

1 NORTH ATLANTIC
2 ATLANTIC
3 GREAT LAKES/UPPER MIDWEST
4 GULF
5 PACIFIC
6 NORTH PACIFIC
7 WESTERN PACIFIC

HAWAII
PACIFIC SOUTHWEST
1:20,000,000

ALASKA
ALASKA
1:64,000,000

GUAM 1:3,000,000
SWAINS ISLAND 1:1,057,307
AMERICAN SAMOA 1:10,000,000
PUERTO RICO 1:6,000,000
SOUTHERN
U.S. VIRGIN ISLANDS

0   500 KILOMETERS
0   500 MILES
1:20,000,000

Map prepared by The Congressional Cartography Program, Geography and Map Division, Library of Congress, 2004

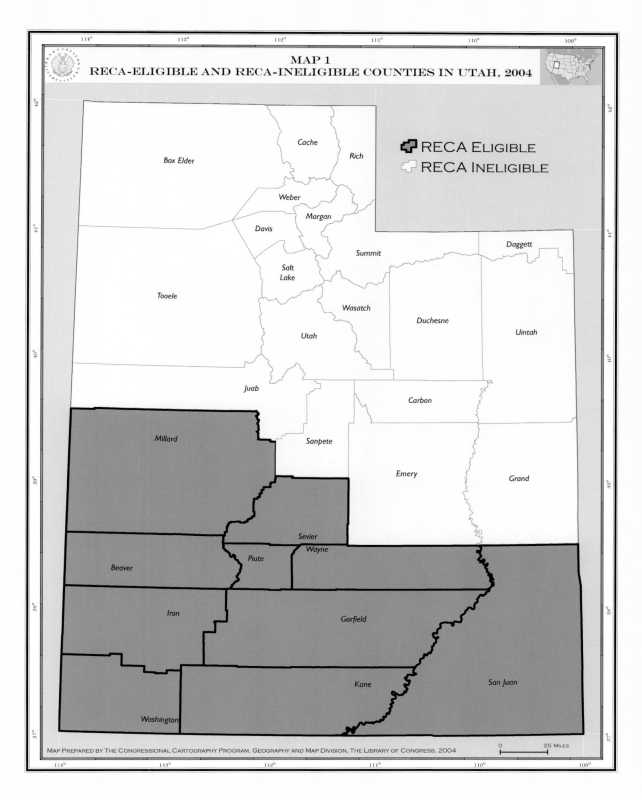

MAP 1
RECA-ELIGIBLE AND RECA-INELIGIBLE COUNTIES IN UTAH, 2004

RECA ELIGIBLE
RECA INELIGIBLE

MAP PREPARED BY THE CONGRESSIONAL CARTOGRAPHY PROGRAM, GEOGRAPHY AND MAP DIVISION, THE LIBRARY OF CONGRESS, 2004

Radiation-Associated Cancer in Utah from 1973 to 2001

From January 1951 to July 1962, the U.S. Atomic Energy Commission conducted nearly one hundred aboveground nuclear detonations at the Nevada Test Site. Nuclear fallout from these tests exposed nearby residents, known as downwinders, to dangerous amounts of radiation. In 1990, the U.S. Congress (House and Senate) passed the Radiation Exposure Compensation Act (RECA) to compensate victims of U.S. nuclear testing. According to the law, residents of ten southwestern counties in Utah are eligible for compensation, while residents of nineteen other Utah counties are ineligible.

These maps were prepared for the Special Investigations Division's examination of cancer rates in Utah. The study looked at new information compiled by the National Cancer Institute that included information about the rates of radiation-associated cancers by county in Utah from 1973 to 2001. The data showed that radiation-associated cancer is actually more common in counties where residents are excluded from compensation than in those counties where residents are included under the RECA law.

The committee's full report is downloadable at www.democrats.reform.house.gov/ Documents/20050413160242-68446.pdf.

Committee on Government Reform—Minority Office Special Investigations Division

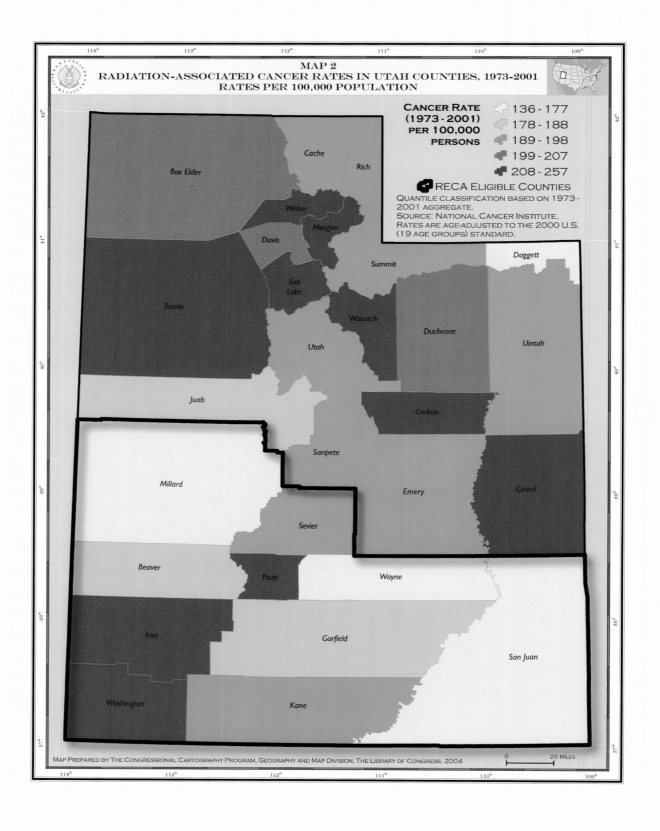

MAP 2
RADIATION-ASSOCIATED CANCER RATES IN UTAH COUNTIES, 1973-2001
RATES PER 100,000 POPULATION

CANCER RATE (1973 - 2001) PER 100,000 PERSONS

136 - 177
178 - 188
189 - 198
199 - 207
208 - 257

RECA ELIGIBLE COUNTIES

QUANTILE CLASSIFICATION BASED ON 1973-2001 AGGREGATE.
SOURCE: NATIONAL CANCER INSTITUTE.
RATES ARE AGE-ADJUSTED TO THE 2000 U.S. (19 AGE GROUPS) STANDARD.

MAP PREPARED BY THE CONGRESSIONAL CARTOGRAPHY PROGRAM, GEOGRAPHY AND MAP DIVISION, THE LIBRARY OF CONGRESS, 2004

25 MILES

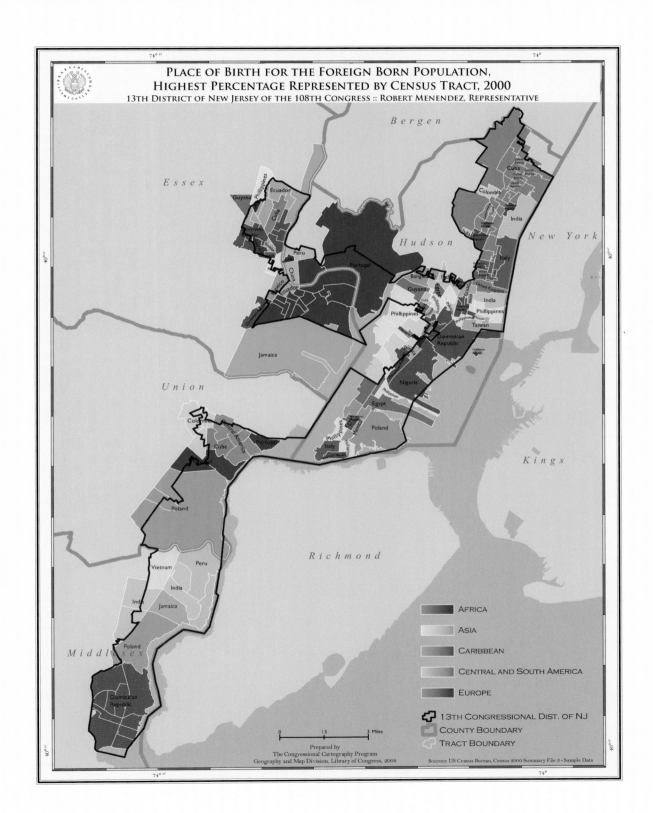

PLACE OF BIRTH FOR THE FOREIGN BORN POPULATION,
HIGHEST PERCENTAGE REPRESENTED BY CENSUS TRACT, 2000
13TH DISTRICT OF NEW JERSEY OF THE 108TH CONGRESS :: ROBERT MENENDEZ, REPRESENTATIVE

AFRICA

ASIA

CARIBBEAN

CENTRAL AND SOUTH AMERICA

EUROPE

13TH CONGRESSIONAL DIST. OF NJ

COUNTY BOUNDARY

TRACT BOUNDARY

Prepared by
The Congressional Cartography Program
Geography and Map Division, Library of Congress, 2004

Sources US Census Bureau, Census 2000 Summary File 3 - Sample Data

Ancestry Maps

This group of maps was created for information purposes for Representative Robert Menendez. He wanted to be able to make appropriate outreach efforts with different ethnic and cultural groups in his district.

Looking through pages and pages of census data for this information was time consuming and tedious, and the information was not in an easy-to-use format. The maps, however, provided this information in a helpful format and enabled Menendez to pinpoint where to focus certain outreach activities.

Representative Robert Menendez (New Jersey 13)

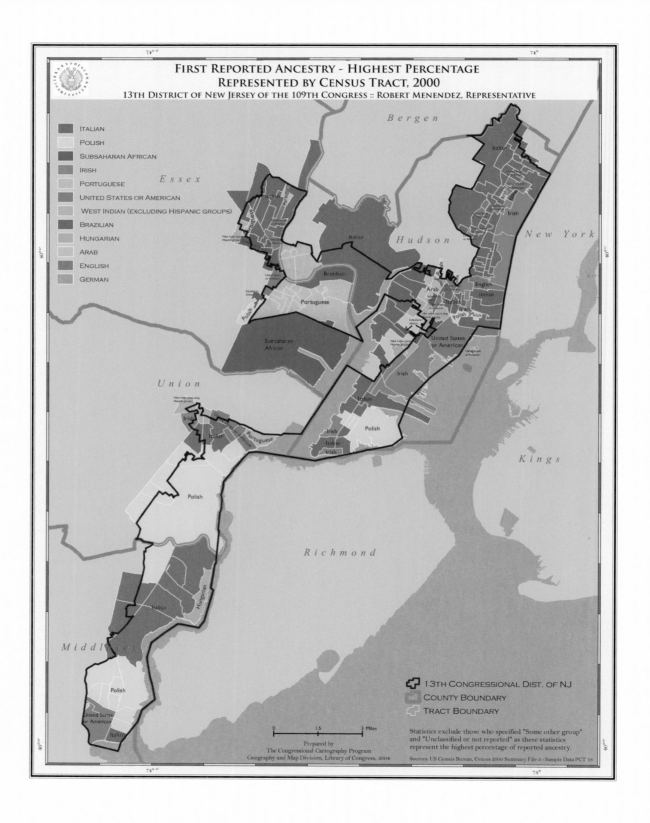

FIRST REPORTED ANCESTRY - HIGHEST PERCENTAGE
REPRESENTED BY CENSUS TRACT, 2000
13TH DISTRICT OF NEW JERSEY OF THE 109TH CONGRESS :: ROBERT MENENDEZ, REPRESENTATIVE

ITALIAN
POLISH
SUBSAHARAN AFRICAN
IRISH
PORTUGUESE
UNITED STATES OR AMERICAN
WEST INDIAN (EXCLUDING HISPANIC GROUPS)
BRAZILIAN
HUNGARIAN
ARAB
ENGLISH
GERMAN

13TH CONGRESSIONAL DIST. OF NJ
COUNTY BOUNDARY
TRACT BOUNDARY

Statistics exclude those who specified "Some other group"
and "Unclassified or not reported" as these statistics
represent the highest percentage of reported ancestry.

Prepared by
The Congressional Cartography Program
Geography and Map Division, Library of Congress, 2004

Sources: US Census Bureau, Census 2000 Summary File 3 - Sample Data PCT 18

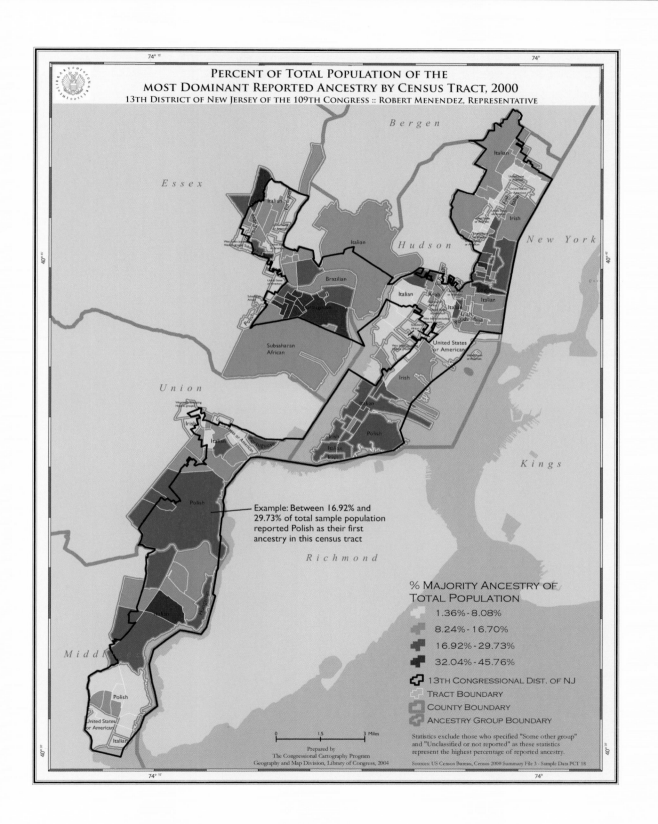

PERCENT OF TOTAL POPULATION OF THE
MOST DOMINANT REPORTED ANCESTRY BY CENSUS TRACT, 2000
13TH DISTRICT OF NEW JERSEY OF THE 109TH CONGRESS :: ROBERT MENENDEZ, REPRESENTATIVE

Example: Between 16.92% and
29.73% of total sample population
reported Polish as their first
ancestry in this census tract

% MAJORITY ANCESTRY OF
TOTAL POPULATION

1.36% - 8.08%
8.24% - 16.70%
16.92% - 29.73%
32.04% - 45.76%

13TH CONGRESSIONAL DIST. OF NJ
TRACT BOUNDARY
COUNTY BOUNDARY
ANCESTRY GROUP BOUNDARY

Statistics exclude those who specified "Some other group"
and "Unclassified or not reported" as these statistics
represent the highest percentage of reported ancestry.

Sources: US Census Bureau, Census 2000 Summary File 3 - Sample Data PCT 18

Prepared by
The Congressional Cartography Program
Geography and Map Division, Library of Congress, 2004

0   1.5   3 Miles

VETERANS HISTORY PROJECT INTERVIEWS IN CALIFORNIA, AS OF MAY, 2005
WITH CONGRESSIONAL DISTRICTS OF THE 109TH CONGRESS OF THE UNITED STATES

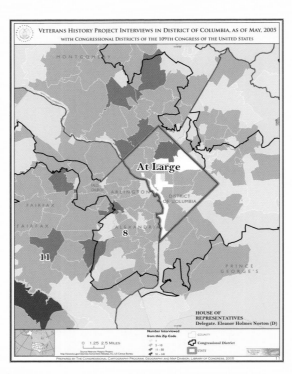

VETERANS HISTORY PROJECT INTERVIEWS IN DISTRICT OF COLUMBIA, AS OF MAY, 2005
WITH CONGRESSIONAL DISTRICTS OF THE 109TH CONGRESS OF THE UNITED STATES

VETERANS HISTORY PROJECT INTERVIEWS IN NEW YORK, AS OF MAY, 2005
WITH CONGRESSIONAL DISTRICTS OF THE 109TH CONGRESS OF THE UNITED STATES

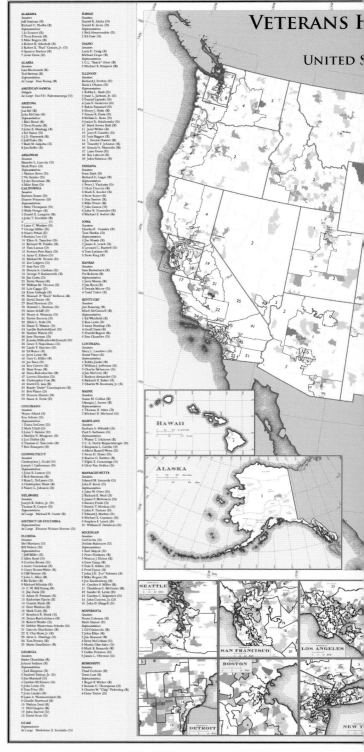

VETERANS H
UNITED S

Veterans History Project
Interview Locations

The U.S. Congress created the Veterans History Project in 2000 as part of the American Folklife Center at the Library of Congress. The project collects and archives the personal recollections of U.S. wartime veterans to honor their service and share their stories with current and future generations.

The primary focus is on firsthand accounts of U.S. veterans from World War I, World War II, the Korean War, the Vietnam War, the Persian Gulf War, and the Afghanistan and Iraq conflicts. In addition, U.S. civilians who were actively involved in supporting war efforts (such as war industry workers, USO workers, flight instructors, and medical volunteers) are also invited to share their valuable stories.

These maps were prepared as part of the Veterans History Project's outreach to ensure the geographic distribution was balanced, evaluate the program's effectiveness, and show how the project reached into communities throughout the United States. It is also important to show members of Congress the project's influence in their communities.

States Losing Amtrak Service Under Committee Plan

In June 2005, when the Transportation Appropriations bill came out of the U.S. House of Representatives' committee, it contained a provision eliminating all of Amtrak's long-distance routes. The effect of the measure was not obvious from the language of the bill, however, which stated, "None of the funds herein shall be available for the operation and maintenance of routes RT16A, RT18, RT19. . . ." When the routes were listed by name in a table (the Cardinal, the Empire Builder), the real impact of the provision was not clear to most members of Congress.

A legislative assistant for New Jersey Congressman Robert Menendez requested a map that showed which states would be affected by the loss of Amtrak service. The resulting map, with eliminated routes in red and eliminated states highlighted in yellow, made a powerful statement during the floor debate. A large version of the map for use on the floor was generated, and members who saw it for the first time were generally taken aback by how much of the country would lose service. A smaller version of the map was provided to House members before the vote on an amendment to restore the long-distance routes.

It is impossible to tell what the vote would have been otherwise, but many believe the map was a crucial factor in getting the amendment to pass by more than 110 votes, a much larger margin than anyone thought possible.

Representative Robert Menendez (New Jersey 13)

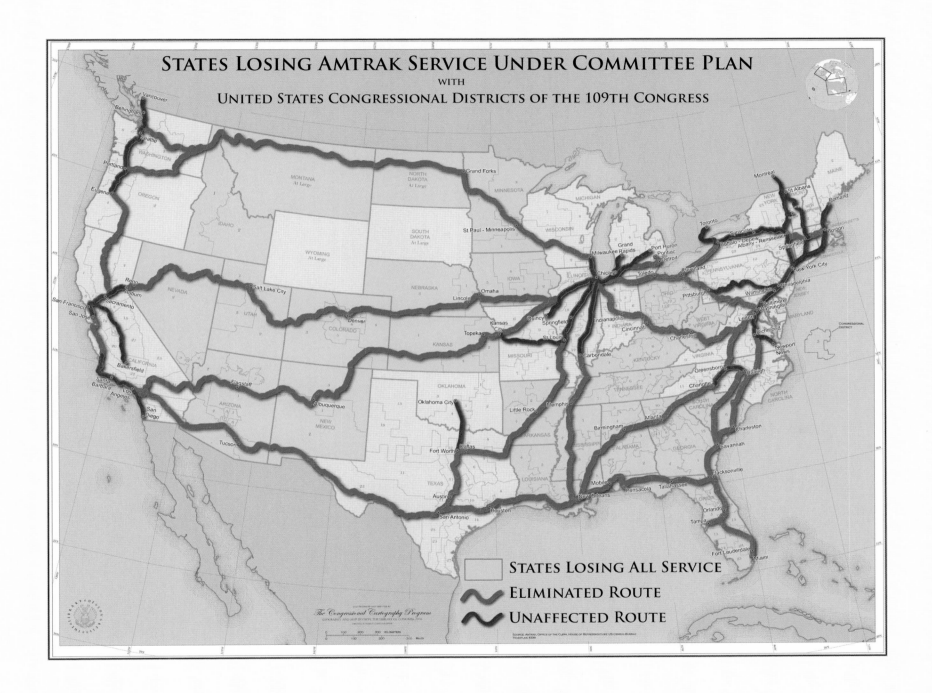

STATES LOSING AMTRAK SERVICE UNDER COMMITTEE PLAN
WITH
UNITED STATES CONGRESSIONAL DISTRICTS OF THE 109TH CONGRESS

STATES LOSING ALL SERVICE

ELIMINATED ROUTE

UNAFFECTED ROUTE

3

Mapping the Course of America's Trends

Mapping the Course of America's Trends

For decades, volumes have been spoken and written about the acquisition, development, application, and value of data. Conflicting viewpoints about methodologies, theories, and usage abound as demographers discover better and faster methods of data gathering and processing. One of the first examples of data gathering in the United States was the count of the U.S. population that began when the first U.S. decennial census was conducted in 1790.

This modest beginning has exploded into a multimillion-dollar industry of marketing information companies that use census data as the basis for developing products, software, and services that deliver data, research, and marketing applications to companies, government agencies, universities, and nonprofit organizations. Software technology innovations and use of the Internet as a conduit have increased the speed of delivery and heightened competition among private-sector data providers.

Accessing Accurate Information

Access to accurate, timely data is critical in today's competitive environment as agencies and organizations search for every advantage. Data users are hungry for the newest and best data while working better, faster, and cheaper.

Making informed decisions requires using accurate and timely data that has been derived from proven, benchmarked methodologies. Primary categories of data collected by public agencies and private companies include business, consumer spending, crime, demographics, media, shopping center, and traffic.

Data categories such as consumer spending and demographics are used to build segmentation systems. For the past thirty years, government agencies and organizations have used segmentation to divide and group markets and more precisely target only certain types of customers, constituents, and prospects. This targeting method is superior to using scattershot methods that might or might not attract preferred groups.

Segmenting Data

Segmentation explains the differences in consumer and constituent types, simplifies marketing campaigns, describes lifestyle and life stage, and incorporates a range of other pertinent information. Segmentation systems operate on the theory that people with similar tastes, lifestyles, and behaviors seek others with the same tastes—"like seeks like." These behaviors can be measured, predicted, and targeted.

The ESRI® segmentation system, Community™ Tapestry™, combines the "who" of lifestyle demography with the "where" of local neighborhood geography to create a model of various lifestyle classifications or segments of actual neighborhoods with addresses—distinct behavioral market segments.

Using proven segmentation methodology introduced more than thirty years ago, Community Tapestry classifies U.S. neighborhoods into sixty-five segments based on their socioeconomic and demographic composition, providing an accurate, detailed description of America's neighborhoods. For a broader view of U.S. neighborhoods, Tapestry further classifies each of the sixty-five segments into two types of summary groups:

- LifeMode: Twelve summary groups based on lifestyle and life stage

- Urbanization: Eleven summary groups based on geographic and physical features and income

Making Public Policy with the Right Data

For years, federal, state, and local government agencies, legislators, and policy makers have depended on this kind of data to bolster their positions on legislative issues. Mixing constituent data with other types of data enables government researchers to provide a more complete picture of people and areas directly and indirectly affected by government programs and issues. Data used in legislative research can help government entities do the following:

- Research the effectiveness of government programs.

- Define underserved areas.

- Study the impact of government programs and services on specific groups.

- Profile the demographics of voters by geography.

- Tailor campaigns and program messaging to the demographics of specific populations.

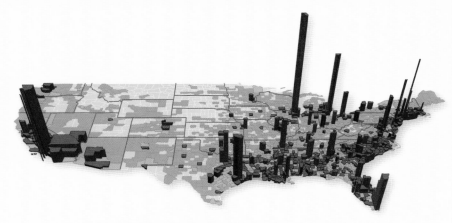

Using three-dimensional mapping, this image shows the population of blacks in America by county. The height of each county (bar) represents the number of blacks in each county.

Looking for the Less Obvious

As you review each of the maps in the following section, try to imagine how different groups, agencies, or organizations might be able to use the map's data for their purposes. While each map illustrates an obvious situation, by looking at them from different perspectives such as accountability and performance measurements, you can see impacts that are not always apparent.

For instance, you can understand how certain regulations, taxes, or legislation can affect different segments of society whether they are smokers, foreign travelers, elderly, or high-technology industry workers. Which areas of the country will be more influenced by the aging baby boom population? Which areas will be impacted by a transportation tax, a tobacco tax, or an Internet commerce tax?

The following map collection examines existing demographic trends in the United States and forecasts some issues that are of interest to government policy makers. Data used to create these maps includes ESRI demographic data; consumer survey data from Mediamark Research Inc., Doublebase 2004; and the ESRI segmentation system Community Tapestry.

In this section of the book, the scale on the maps is ranked low, medium, and high and shows either the actual percentage of the population by ZIP Code that is represented in a category or demographic description or a scale that is related to the ranking of each ZIP Code in the category.

Trends in American Health Care

Public policy is one of the most important factors in guiding change in America's health care system. Issues such as accessible, affordable, and high-quality health care; outbreaks of new diseases; chronic conditions that reach epidemic proportions; and the lack of insurance coverage exert stress on health care delivery systems and require health policy initiatives that will reduce or prevent failures in the health care market.

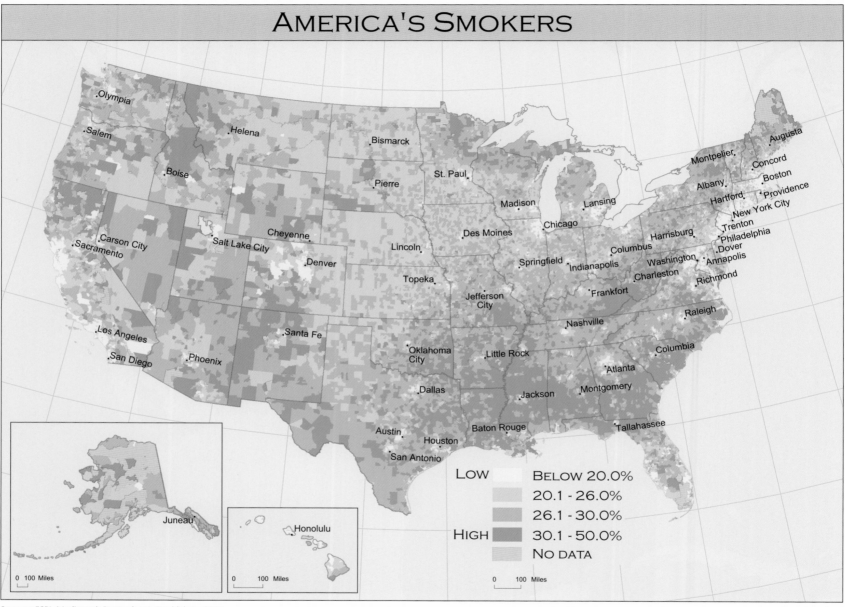

AMERICA'S SMOKERS

Olympia
Salem
Helena
Bismarck
Boise
St. Paul
Pierre
Madison
Lansing
Montpelier
Augusta
Concord
Boston
Albany
Hartford
Providence
New York City
Cheyenne
Salt Lake City
Lincoln
Des Moines
Chicago
Harrisburg
Trenton
Philadelphia
Carson City
Denver
Springfield
Indianapolis
Columbus
Dover
Sacramento
Topeka
Washington
Annapolis
Charleston
Richmond
Jefferson City
Frankfort
Los Angeles
Santa Fe
Nashville
Raleigh
San Diego
Phoenix
Oklahoma City
Little Rock
Columbia
Atlanta
Dallas
Jackson
Montgomery
Austin
Baton Rouge
Tallahassee
Houston
San Antonio

Juneau

Honolulu

LOW — BELOW 20.0%
20.1 - 26.0%
26.1 - 30.0%
HIGH — 30.1 - 50.0%
NO DATA

0 100 Miles

0 100 Miles

0 100 Miles

Sources: ESRI, Mediamark Research Inc. Doublebase 2004

America's Smokers

This map shows adults who smoked cigarettes over a twelve-month period as a percentage of the total adult population.

PRESCRIPTION DRUG USERS

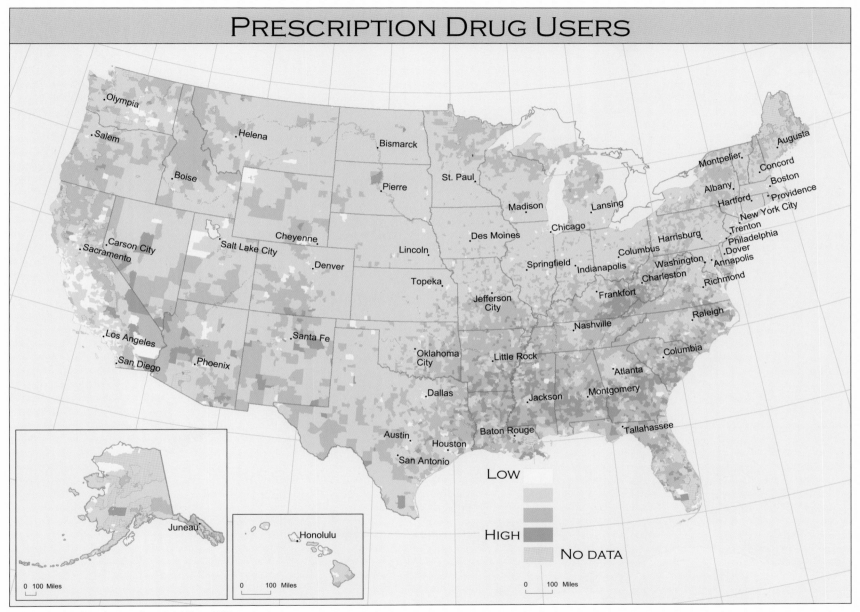

LOW

HIGH

NO DATA

Sources: ESRI, Mediamark Research Inc. Doublebase 2003

Prescription Drug Users

This map shows areas in the United States where adults who use prescription drugs are located based on the number of adult users per ZIP Code.

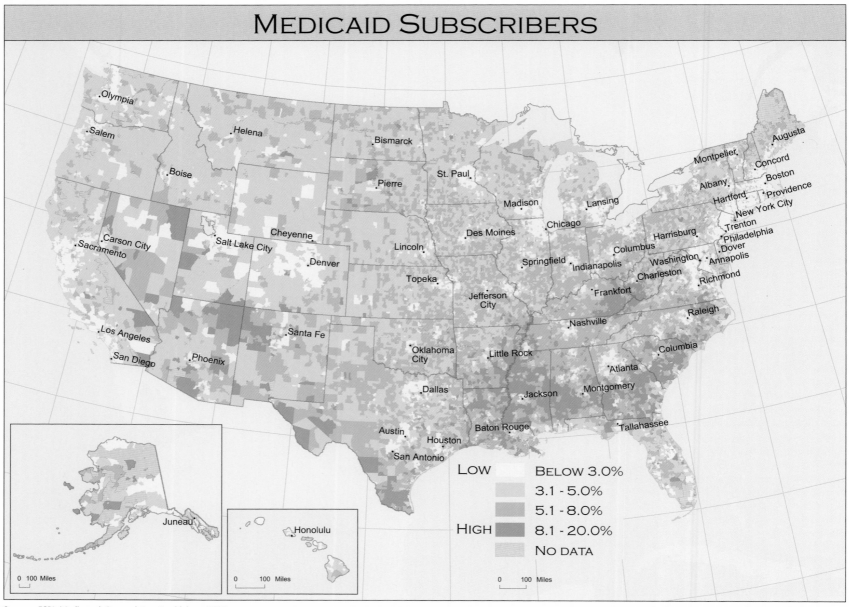

MEDICAID SUBSCRIBERS

LOW — BELOW 3.0%

3.1 - 5.0%

5.1 - 8.0%

HIGH — 8.1 - 20.0%

NO DATA

Sources: ESRI, Mediamark Research Inc. Doublebase 2004

Medicaid Enrollees

This map depicts, by population percentages, the locations of people in the United States who enroll in Medicaid.

VISITED DOCTOR IN LAST 12 MONTHS

LOW

	BELOW 72.0%
	72.1 - 79.0%
	79.1 - 82.0%
HIGH		82.1 - 89.0%
	NO DATA

Sources: ESRI, Mediamark Research Inc. Doublebase 2004

Visited Doctor in Last 12 Months

This map depicts areas of the United States where adults visited a doctor over the course of twelve months as a percentage of the total adult population.

HEALTH INSURED BY EMPLOYER

Olympia
Salem
Helena
Boise
Bismarck
St. Paul
Pierre
Madison
Lansing
Cheyenne
Salt Lake City
Carson City
Sacramento
Lincoln
Des Moines
Chicago
Denver
Topeka
Springfield
Indianapolis
Columbus
Harrisburg
Los Angeles
Santa Fe
Jefferson City
Frankfort
Charleston
San Diego
Phoenix
Oklahoma City
Little Rock
Nashville
Montpelier
Concord
Augusta
Albany
Boston
Hartford
Providence
New York City
Trenton
Philadelphia
Dover
Washington
Annapolis
Richmond
Raleigh
Columbia
Atlanta
Montgomery
Dallas
Jackson
Austin
Houston
Baton Rouge
San Antonio
Tallahassee
Juneau
Honolulu

LOW   BELOW 36.0%
       36.1 - 43.0%
       43.1 - 50.0%
HIGH   50.1 - 65.0%
       NO DATA

0 100 Miles
0 100 Miles
0 100 Miles

Sources: ESRI, Mediamark Research Inc. Doublebase 2004

Health Insured by Employer

This map illustrates the percentage of adults who obtained medical insurance from their place of work, based on the total adult population.

Growing Old in America

The percentage of older Americans will increase rapidly as the first of the United States' seventy-six million baby boomers turn sixty in 2006 and begin to redefine retirement. This population transformation will affect many issues including social programs, public and private health insurance systems, retirement plans, worker productivity, community planning, and transportation infrastructure.

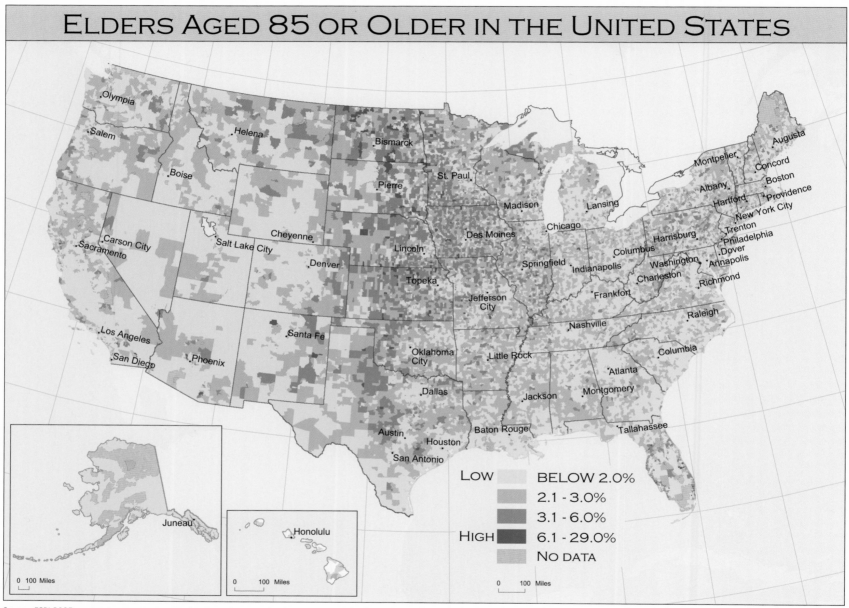

ELDERS AGED 85 OR OLDER IN THE UNITED STATES

Olympia
Salem
Helena
Bismarck
Augusta
Boise
Montpelier
Concord
Pierre
St. Paul
Albany
Boston
Cheyenne
Madison
Lansing
Hartford
Providence
Carson City
Des Moines
Chicago
New York City
Sacramento
Salt Lake City
Lincoln
Harrisburg
Trenton
Denver
Springfield
Columbus
Philadelphia
Topeka
Indianapolis
Washington
Dover
Jefferson City
Frankfort
Charleston
Annapolis
Santa Fe
Richmond
Los Angeles
Nashville
Raleigh
San Diego
Phoenix
Oklahoma City
Little Rock
Columbia
Dallas
Atlanta
Austin
Jackson
Montgomery
Houston
Baton Rouge
Tallahassee
San Antonio

Juneau
Honolulu

LOW   BELOW 2.0%
          2.1 - 3.0%
          3.1 - 6.0%
HIGH 6.1 - 29.0%
          NO DATA

0   100 Miles
0   100 Miles
0   100 Miles

Source: ESRI 2005

Elders Aged 85 or Older in the United States

The locations and population percentages of elders aged eighty-five or older in the United States are shown in this map.

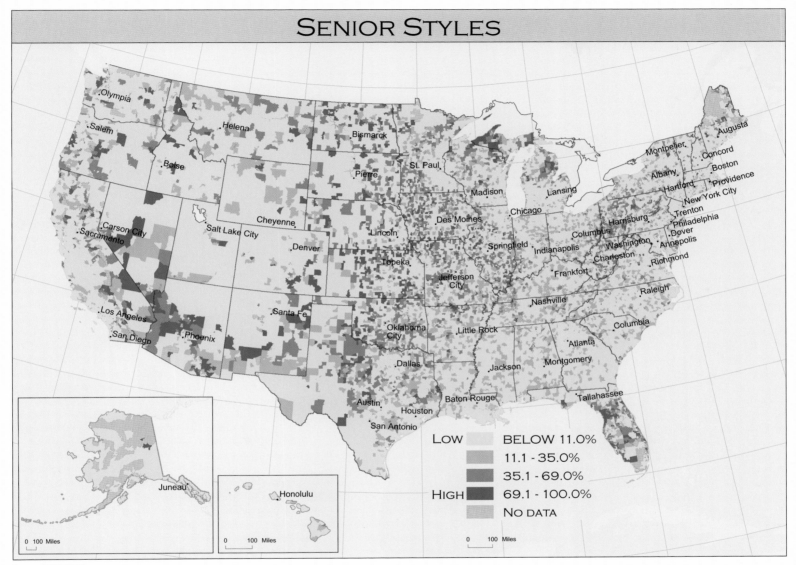

SENIOR STYLES

LOW	BELOW 11.0%
	11.1 - 35.0%
	35.1 - 69.0%
HIGH	69.1 - 100.0%
	NO DATA

Source: ESRI 2005

Senior Styles

This map illustrates the locations of residents who fit Community Tapestry's LifeMode summary group descriptions of the nine "senior" segments. Senior Styles segments point out the diversity among today's senior markets. Younger, more affluent seniors, freed from their child-rearing responsibilities, are traveling and relocating to warmer climates. Settled seniors are anticipating retirement and remaining in their homes. This is the most politically active of Community Tapestry's summary groups, from voting to participating in election campaigns.

RUSTBELT RETIREES

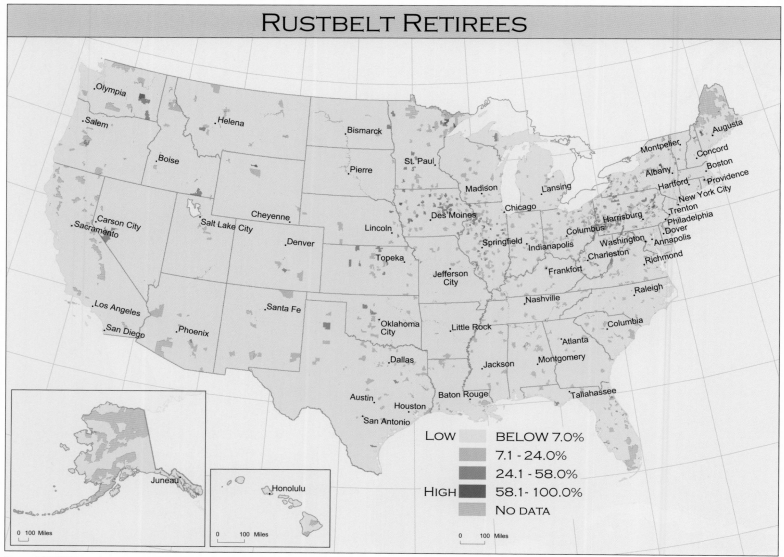

LOW	BELOW 7.0%
	7.1 - 24.0%
	24.1 - 58.0%
HIGH	58.1 - 100.0%
	NO DATA

Source: ESRI 2005

Rustbelt Retirees

Locations of neighborhoods that fit the description of the Rustbelt Retirees segment, part of ESRI's Community Tapestry segmentation system, are shown in this map. Most Rustbelt Retirees neighborhoods can be found in older, industrial northeastern cities and states surrounding the Great Lakes. Married couples with no children and singles who live alone comprise most of the household types in Rustbelt Retirees neighborhoods. Loyal to their country and communities, Rustbelt Retirees residents participate in volunteer and fund-raising work, visit elected officials, and work for political parties or candidates.

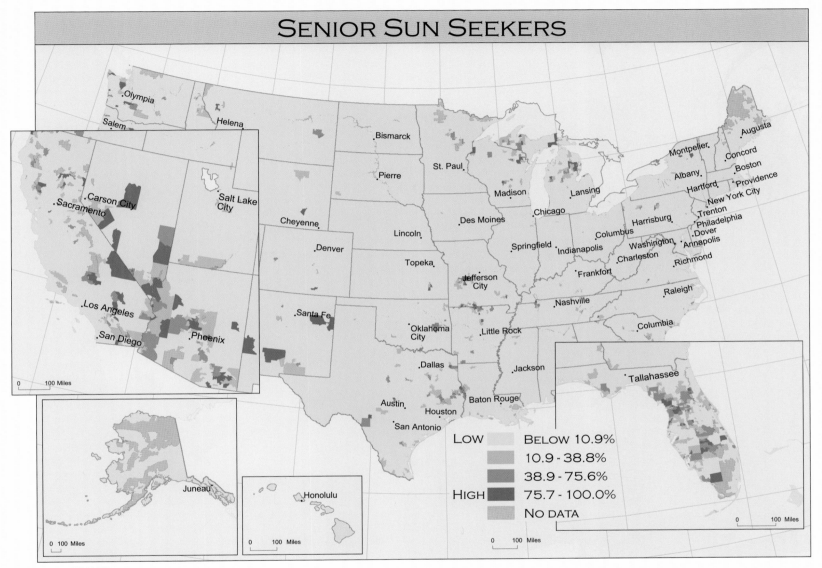

SENIOR SUN SEEKERS

Olympia
Salem
Helena
Bismarck
St. Paul
Pierre
Madison
Lansing
Augusta
Montpelier
Concord
Albany
Boston
Hartford
Providence
New York City
Carson City
Sacramento
Salt Lake City
Cheyenne
Des Moines
Chicago
Trenton
Philadelphia
Dover
Lincoln
Harrisburg
Columbus
Springfield
Indianapolis
Washington
Annapolis
Denver
Charleston
Richmond
Los Angeles
Topeka
Jefferson City
Frankfort
San Diego
Phoenix
Raleigh
Santa Fe
Nashville
Oklahoma City
Little Rock
Columbia
Dallas
Jackson
Tallahassee
Austin
Baton Rouge
Houston
San Antonio
Juneau
Honolulu

LOW   BELOW 10.9%
10.9 - 38.8%
38.9 - 75.6%
HIGH   75.7 - 100.0%
NO DATA

0   100 Miles

Source: ESRI 2005

Senior Sun Seekers

This trio of maps illustrates the locations of Community Tapestry's Senior Sun Seekers neighborhoods in the United States and areas where these neighborhoods are concentrated. Senior Sun Seekers is one of the faster-growing markets and, with a median age of 51.4 years, the third-oldest population of all Community Tapestry segments. Many residents are retired or are anticipating retirement; more than half of these households receive Social Security benefits. Located mostly in the South and West to escape cold winters, favorite areas are Florida and portions of Arizona and California.

MEDICARE BENEFICIARIES

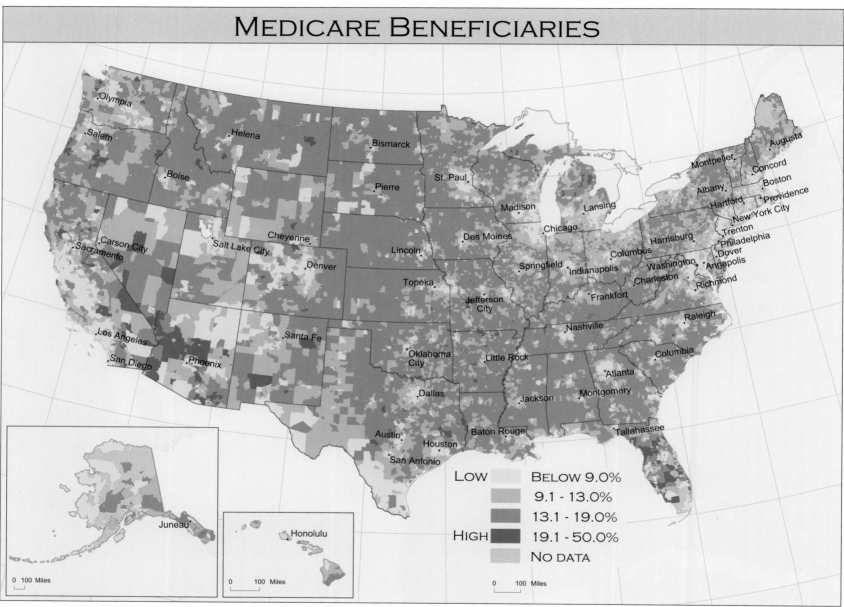

Olympia
Salem
Helena
Boise
Bismarck
Pierre
St. Paul
Cheyenne
Salt Lake City
Madison
Lansing
Chicago
Montpelier
Concord
Boston
Albany
Hartford
Providence
New York City
Carson City
Sacramento
Denver
Lincoln
Des Moines
Harrisburg
Trenton
Philadelphia
Columbus
Dover
Springfield
Indianapolis
Washington
Annapolis
Topeka
Charleston
Richmond
Los Angeles
Santa Fe
Jefferson City
Frankfort
San Diego
Phoenix
Oklahoma City
Little Rock
Nashville
Raleigh
Dallas
Columbia
Atlanta
Austin
Jackson
Montgomery
Houston
Baton Rouge
Tallahassee
San Antonio

Juneau

Honolulu

Low   BELOW 9.0%
       9.1 - 13.0%
       13.1 - 19.0%
HIGH   19.1 - 50.0%
       NO DATA

0 100 Miles
0 100 Miles
0 100 Miles

Sources: ESRI, Mediamark Research Inc. Doublebase 2004

Medicare Beneficiaries

This map illustrates the locations of adults in the United States who benefit from Medicare as a percentage of the total adult population.

American High Technology

First came PCs, then smaller, faster microprocessors; the Internet; and cell phones—all have done their part to revolutionize our everyday lives, how we use information, and how we disseminate it. Easier and faster access to information enables an ongoing dialog between public officials and their constituents and brings to the fore issues that might not have been expected or previously explored.

INFORMATION INDUSTRY WORKERS

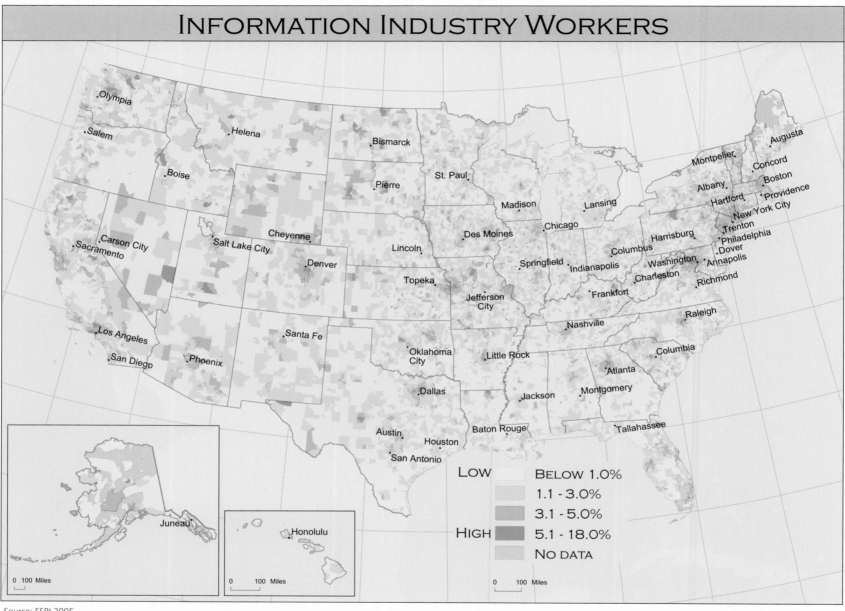

LOW · BELOW 1.0%
· 1.1 - 3.0%
· 3.1 - 5.0%
HIGH · 5.1 - 18.0%
· NO DATA

Source: ESRI 2005

Information Industry Workers

The locations of information industry workers in the United States as a percentage of all employed persons are shown in this map.

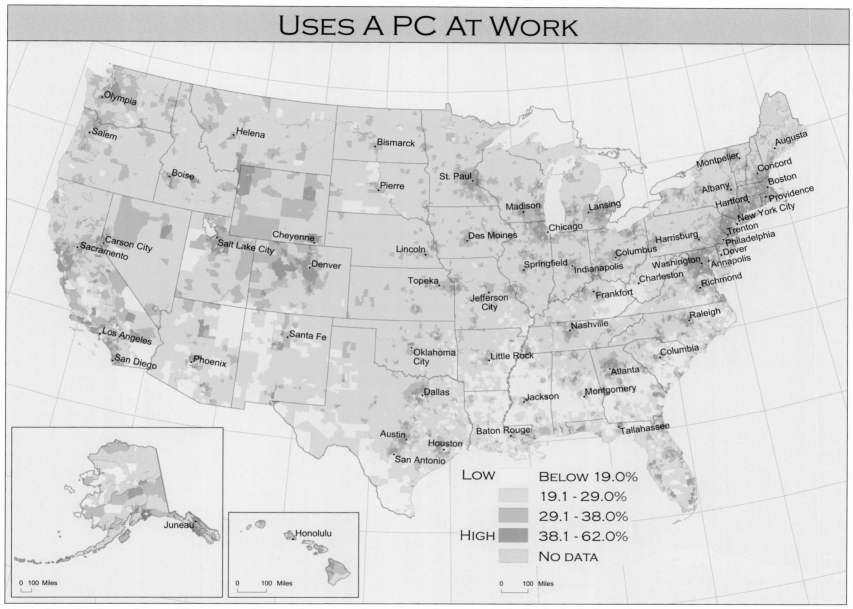

USES A PC AT WORK

LOW — BELOW 19.0%
19.1 - 29.0%
29.1 - 38.0%
HIGH — 38.1 - 62.0%
NO DATA

Sources: ESRI, Mediamark Research Inc. Doublebase 2004

Uses a PC at Work

This map illustrates the locations of U.S adults who use personal computers at work as a percentage of the entire adult population.

HOUSEHOLD OWNS A PC

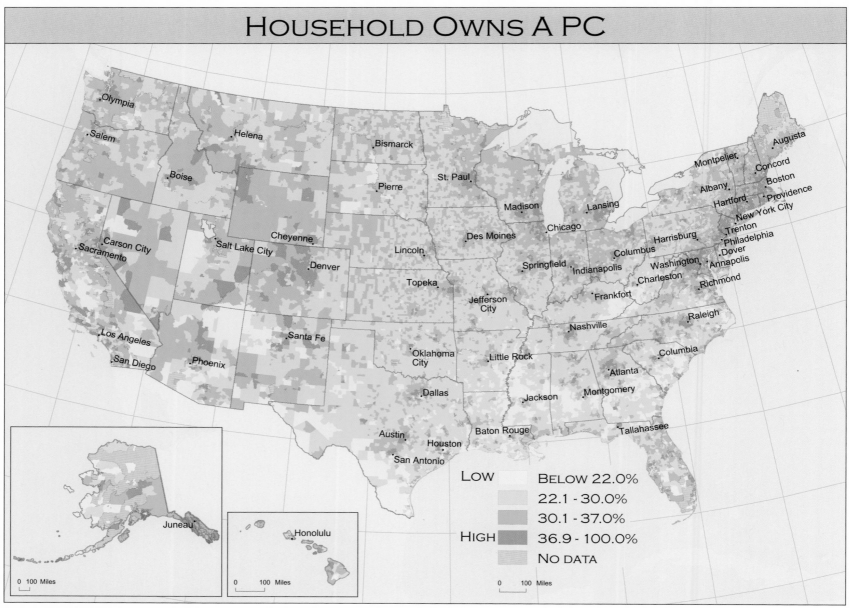

LOW BELOW 22.0%
22.1 - 30.0%
30.1 - 37.0%
HIGH 36.9 - 100.0%
NO DATA

Sources: ESRI, Mediamark Research Inc. Doublebase 2004

Household Owns a PC

This map illustrates, by population percentages, areas of the United States where a personal computer is owned by a household.

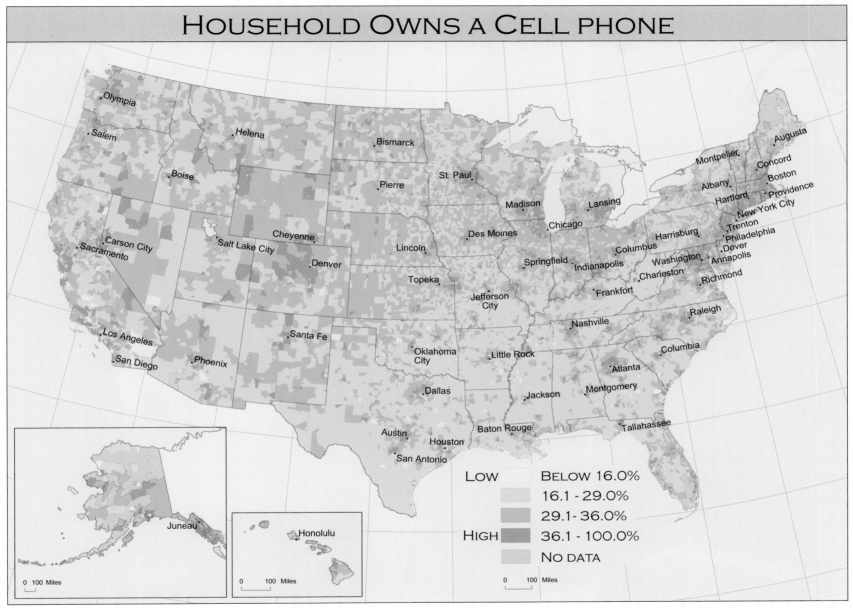

HOUSEHOLD OWNS A CELL PHONE

LOW · BELOW 16.0%
16.1 - 29.0%
29.1- 36.0%
HIGH · 36.1 - 100.0%
NO DATA

Sources: ESRI, Mediamark Research Inc. Doublebase 2003

Household Owns a Cell Phone

This map illustrates locations, by population percentages, of households that own a cell phone in the United States.

ONLINE SHOPPERS

LOW   BELOW 18.0%
         18.1 - 24.0%
         24.1 - 33.0%
HIGH   33.1 - 52.0%
         NO DATA

Sources: ESRI, Mediamark Research Inc. Doublebase 2004

Online Shoppers

This map illustrates, by population percentages, areas where adults shopped online over a twelve-month period.

America's Population Dynamics

Regionally, America's population is growing at different rates. Rapid growth in some areas will increase demand for public services, strain existing systems, and tap affordable housing markets and critical workforces. In addition, population changes will cause political power shifts. Trends in the country's ethnic diversity will also affect public policy in various fields such as education, health care, and job training.

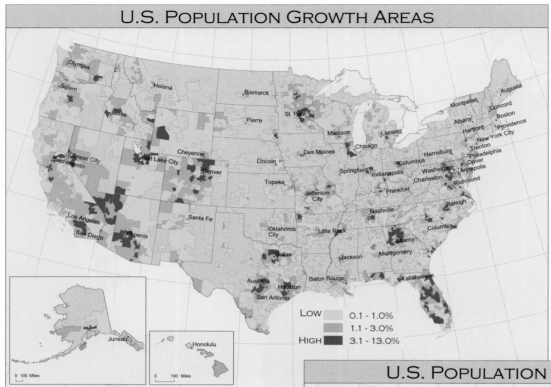

U.S. POPULATION GROWTH AREAS

LOW | 0.1 - 1.0%
| 1.1 - 3.0%
HIGH | 3.1 - 13.0%

Source: ESRI 2005

U.S. Population Growth Areas

This map illustrates the areas of projected population growth in the United States between 2005 and 2010.

Source: ESRI 2005

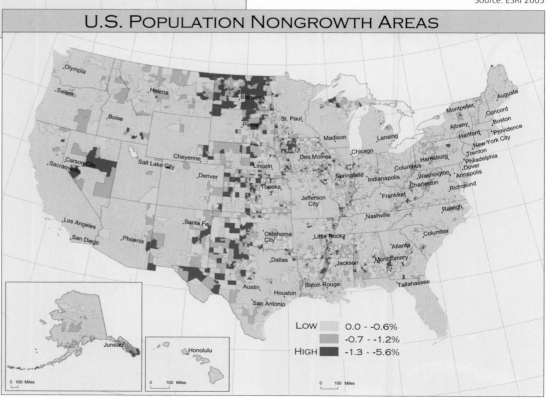

U.S. POPULATION NONGROWTH AREAS

LOW | 0.0 - -0.6%
| -0.7 - -1.2%
HIGH | -1.3 - -5.6%

U.S. Population Nongrowth Areas

In contrast, this map shows areas of the United States where no population growth is projected between 2005 and 2010.

GLOBAL ROOTS

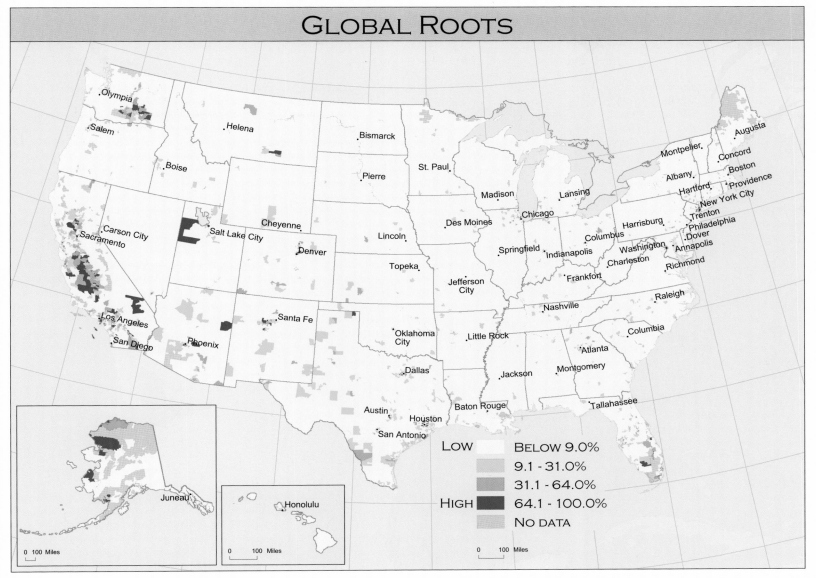

LOW	BELOW 9.0%
	9.1 - 31.0%
	31.1 - 64.0%
HIGH	64.1 - 100.0%
	NO DATA

Source: ESRI 2005

Global Roots

Locations of the segments in Community Tapestry's Global Roots LifeMode summary group in the United States are shown here. The common thread among these segments is ethnic diversity. Global Roots households are young with modest incomes and tend to rent in multiunit buildings. The household types range from married couples, typically with children, to single parents to individuals who live alone. Half of these households have immigrated to the United States within the past ten years.

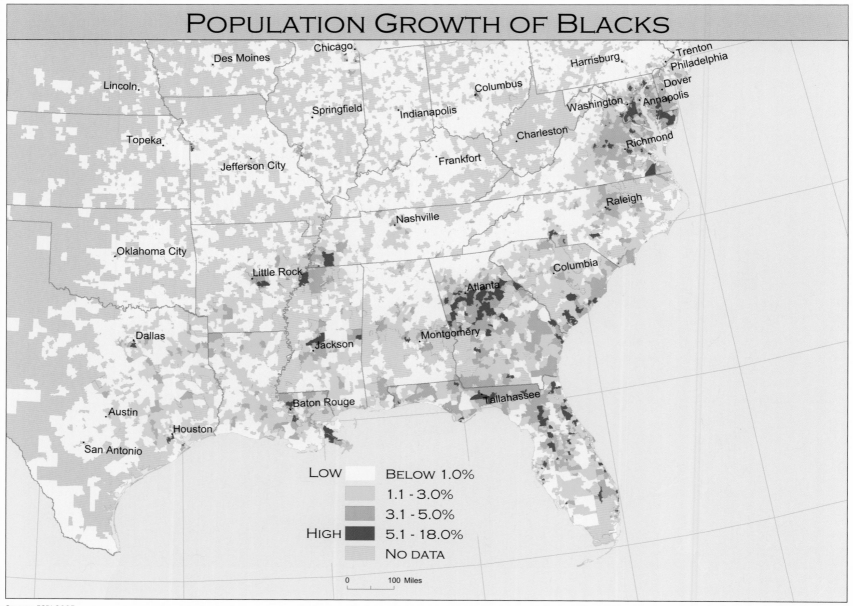

POPULATION GROWTH OF BLACKS

LOW — BELOW 1.0%
1.1 - 3.0%
3.1 - 5.0%
HIGH — 5.1 - 18.0%
NO DATA

0   100 Miles

Source: ESRI 2005

Population Growth of Blacks

The projected percentages of growth in the black population in the southeastern United States for 2005–2010 are illustrated in this map.

POPULATION GROWTH OF HISPANICS

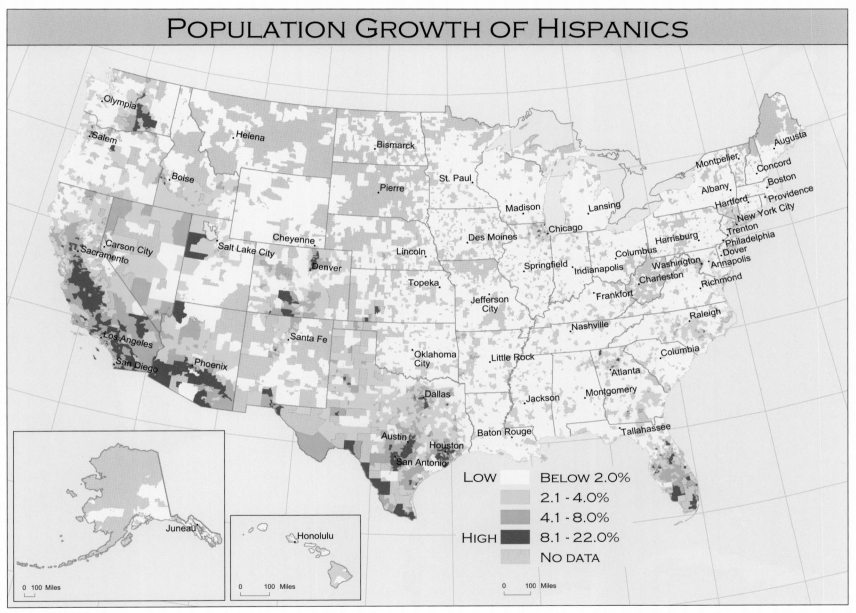

LOW | BELOW 2.0%
| 2.1 - 4.0%
| 4.1 - 8.0%
HIGH | 8.1 - 22.0%
| NO DATA

Source: ESRI 2005

Population Growth of Hispanics

The projected percentages of growth in the Hispanic population in the United States between 2005 and 2010 are illustrated in this map.

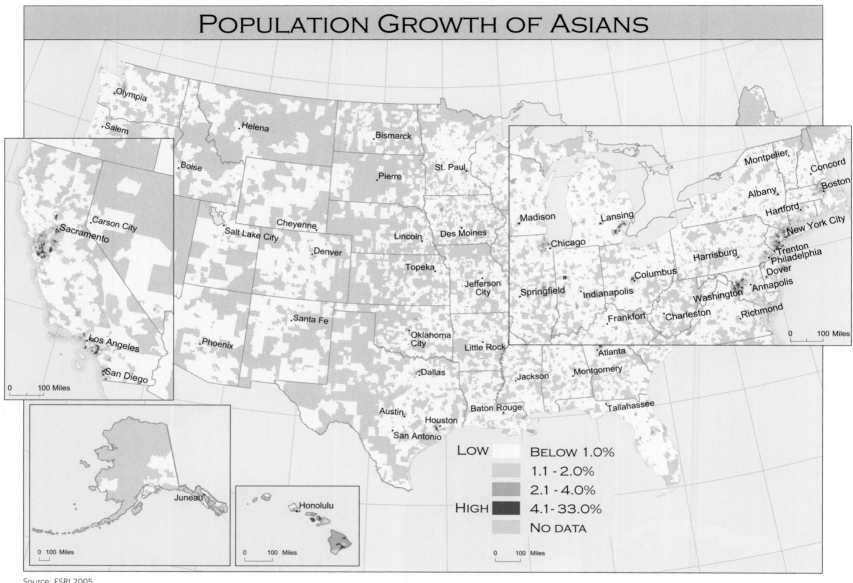

POPULATION GROWTH OF ASIANS

LOW — BELOW 1.0%
1.1 - 2.0%
2.1 - 4.0%
HIGH — 4.1- 33.0%
NO DATA

Source: ESRI 2005

Population Growth of Asians

This trio of maps illustrates where the Asian population is projected to grow between 2005 and 2010 in the United States, as well as areas where the Asian population is concentrated.

Getting from Place to Place

Crisscrossed with highways, railways, subways, ports, and air routes, many of America's major cities are hubs for national and international travel and commerce and are subject to governmental regulation. Moving people and goods safely and efficiently is one of the challenges that local, state, and federal officials face as they seek to find innovative approaches to transportation problem solving.

DOMESTIC TRAVELERS

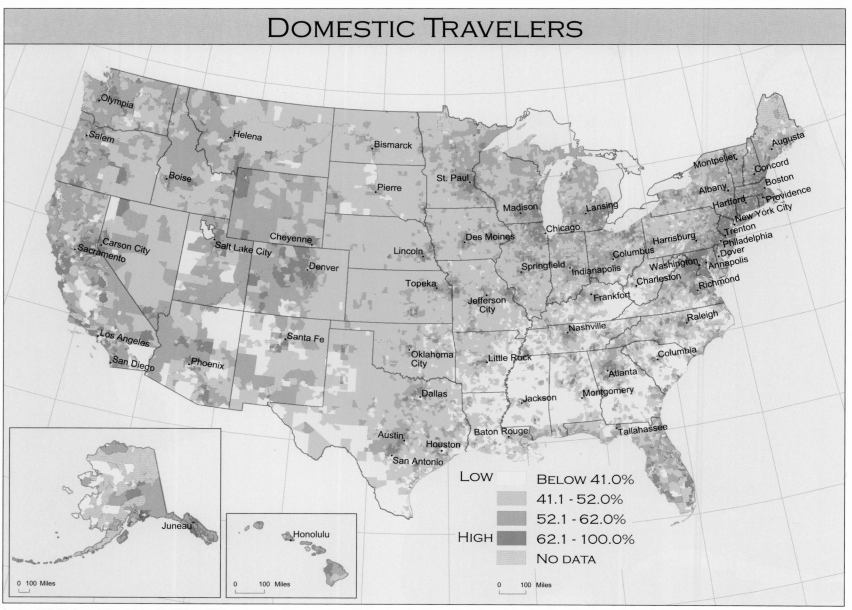

LOW | BELOW 41.0%
| 41.1 - 52.0%
| 52.1 - 62.0%
HIGH | 62.1 - 100.0%
| NO DATA

Sources: ESRI, Mediamark Research Inc. Doublebase 2004

Domestic Travelers

The percentages of adults in the United States who traveled domestically over the course of twelve months are shown in this map.

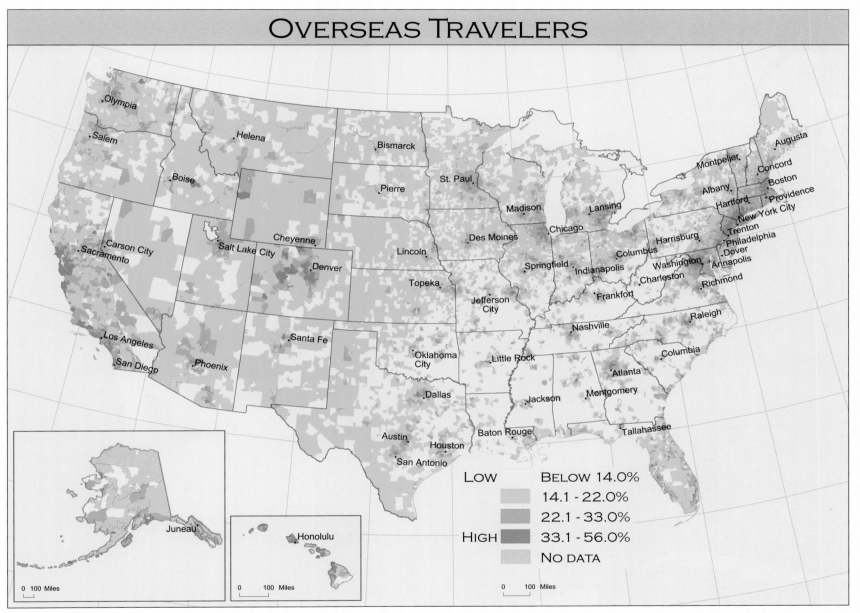

OVERSEAS TRAVELERS

Olympia
Salem
Helena
Bismarck
Boise
St. Paul
Pierre
Madison
Lansing
Augusta
Montpelier
Concord
Boston
Albany
Hartford
Providence
New York City
Carson City
Sacramento
Salt Lake City
Cheyenne
Denver
Lincoln
Des Moines
Chicago
Harrisburg
Columbus
Trenton
Philadelphia
Dover
Springfield
Indianapolis
Washington
Annapolis
Topeka
Charleston
Richmond
Jefferson City
Frankfort
Los Angeles
Santa Fe
Raleigh
San Diego
Nashville
Phoenix
Oklahoma City
Little Rock
Columbia
Dallas
Atlanta
Jackson
Montgomery
Austin
Baton Rouge
Tallahassee
Houston
San Antonio

Juneau
Honolulu

LOW   BELOW 14.0%
       14.1 - 22.0%
       22.1 - 33.0%
HIGH   33.1 - 56.0%
       NO DATA

0 100 Miles
0 100 Miles
0 100 Miles

Sources: ESRI, Mediamark Research Inc. Doublebase 2004

Overseas Travelers

This map shows areas in the United States that are home to adults who engaged in foreign travel during a period of three years.

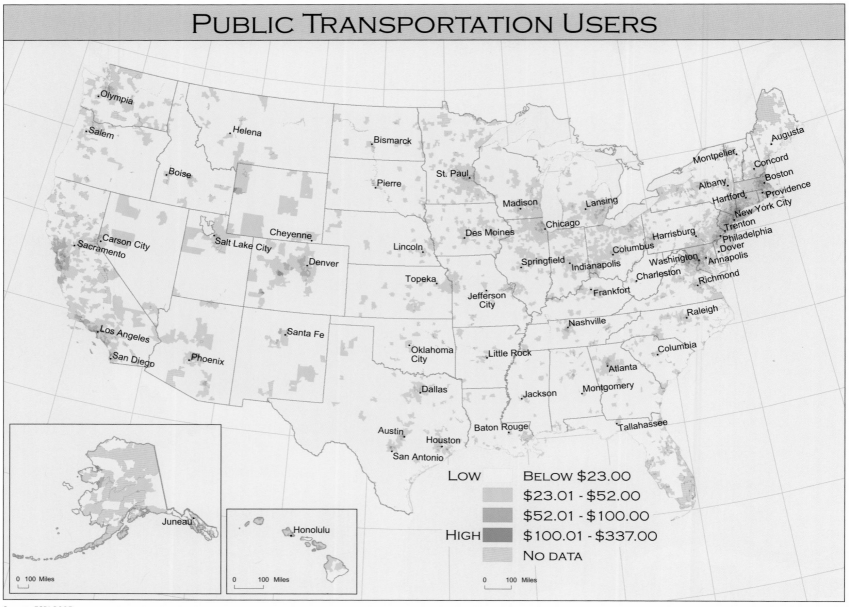

PUBLIC TRANSPORTATION USERS

LOW	BELOW $23.00
	$23.01 - $52.00
	$52.01 - $100.00
HIGH	$100.01 - $337.00
	NO DATA

Source: ESRI 2005

Public Transportation Users

This map illustrates areas in the United States where people use public transportation based on the amount spent yearly by households in the area.

COMMUTES 20 OR MORE MINUTES TO WORK

LOW   BELOW 19.0%
             19.1 - 29.0%
             29.1 - 38.0%
HIGH   38.1 - 67.0%
             NO DATA

0 100 Miles

Source: Census 2000

Commutes 20 or More Minutes to Work

This map illustrates, by population percentages, areas in the United States where people over the age of sixteen commuted twenty or more minutes to work.

Impacts on the Economy

Changes in America's workforce, the population's relationship with money and credit, and shifts in industries can have tremendous impacts on the nation's economy. Standard of living indexes, taxation policies, and funding for research and development are some issues that government agencies consider when they seek to develop policies that foster economic growth and ensure a prosperous future for citizens.

401(K) PARTICIPANTS

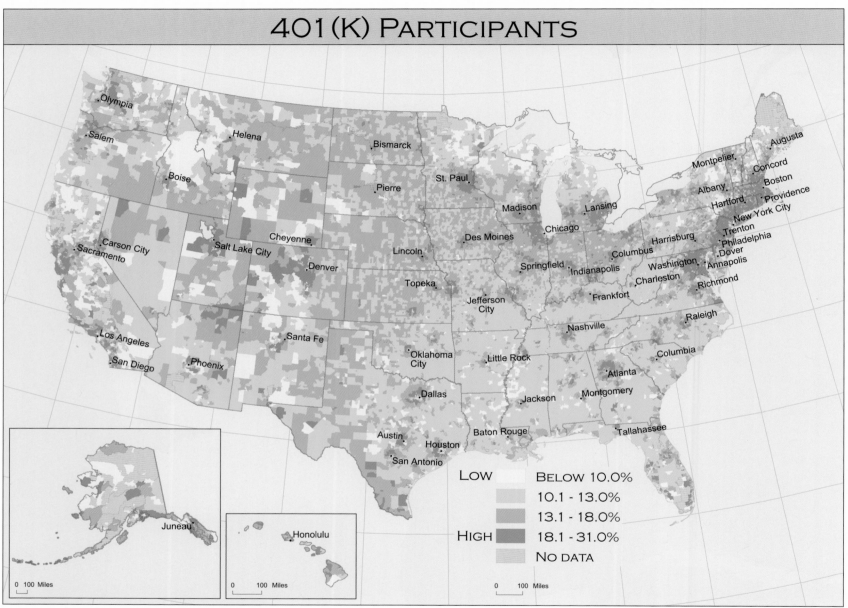

LOW   BELOW 10.0%
           10.1 - 13.0%
           13.1 - 18.0%
HIGH   18.1 - 31.0%
           NO DATA

Sources: ESRI, Mediamark Research Inc. Doublebase 2004

401(k) Participants

This map shows the locations and population percentages of U.S. adults who have 401(k) retirement savings.

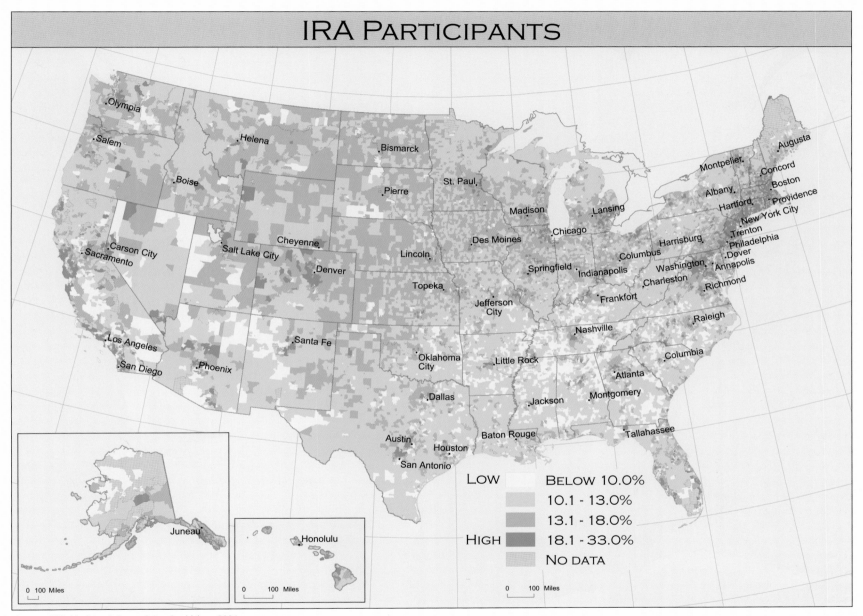

IRA PARTICIPANTS

LOW

	BELOW 10.0%
	10.1 - 13.0%
	13.1 - 18.0%
	18.1 - 33.0%
	NO DATA

HIGH

Sources: ESRI, Mediamark Research Inc. Doublebase 2004

IRA Participants

This map shows the locations and population percentages of U.S. adults who contribute to IRA accounts.

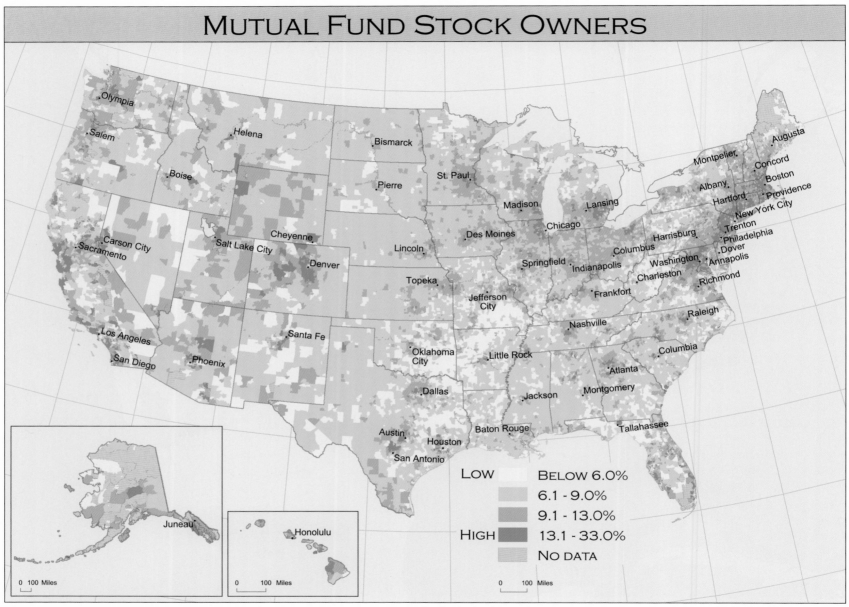

MUTUAL FUND STOCK OWNERS

LOW		BELOW 6.0%
		6.1 - 9.0%
		9.1 - 13.0%
HIGH		13.1 - 33.0%
		NO DATA

Sources: ESRI, Mediamark Research Inc. Doublebase 2004

Mutual Fund Stock Owners

This map shows the locations and population percentages of U.S. adults who own mutual fund stocks.

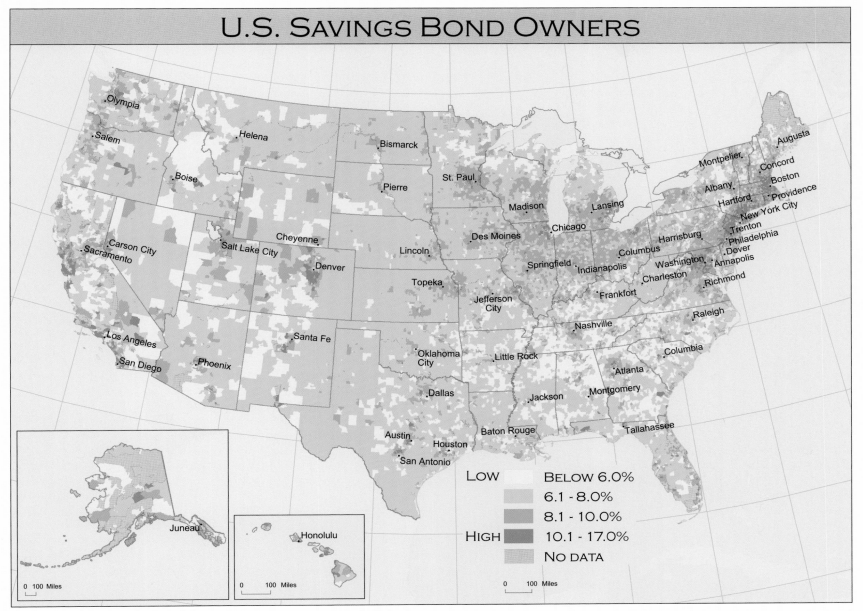

U.S. SAVINGS BOND OWNERS

LOW — BELOW 6.0%
6.1 - 8.0%
8.1 - 10.0%
HIGH — 10.1 - 17.0%
NO DATA

Sources: ESRI, Mediamark Research Inc. Doublebase 2004

U.S. Savings Bond Owners

This map shows the locations and population percentages of U.S. adults who own U.S. savings bonds.

America in Cap and Gown

As globalization takes root and the United States shifts from a manufacturing- to a service-based economy, education, knowledge, and innovation will become driving forces in this transformation. More Americans are graduating from college and taking advantage of lifelong learning opportunities, increasing the need for institutions to expand their programs and meet the needs of students.

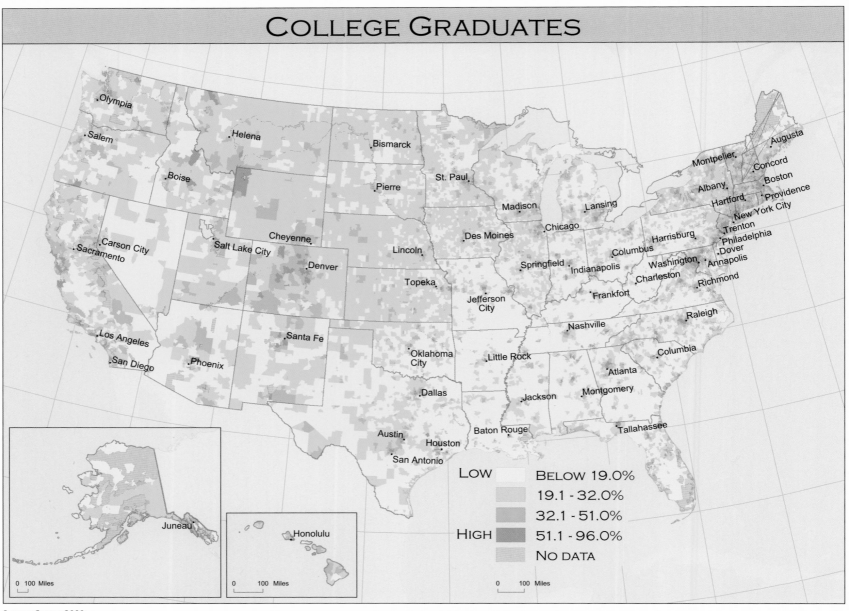

COLLEGE GRADUATES

Olympia
Salem
Helena
Bismarck
Boise
St. Paul
Pierre
Madison
Lansing
Cheyenne
Des Moines
Chicago
Carson City
Salt Lake City
Lincoln
Sacramento
Denver
Topeka
Los Angeles
Santa Fe
Jefferson City
Nashville
San Diego
Phoenix
Oklahoma City
Little Rock
Dallas
Atlanta
Austin
Jackson
Montgomery
Houston
Baton Rouge
Tallahassee
San Antonio

Montpelier
Augusta
Concord
Albany
Boston
Hartford
Providence
New York City
Trenton
Harrisburg
Columbus
Philadelphia
Springfield
Indianapolis
Washington
Dover
Annapolis
Charleston
Richmond
Frankfort
Raleigh
Columbia

Juneau
Honolulu

LOW   BELOW 19.0%
       19.1 - 32.0%
       32.1 - 51.0%
HIGH   51.1 - 96.0%
       NO DATA

0 100 Miles
0 100 Miles
0 100 Miles

Source: Census 2000

College Graduates

This map shows areas where college graduates are found in the United States as a percentage of the population of people aged twenty-five years and older.

DID NOT GRADUATE HIGH SCHOOL

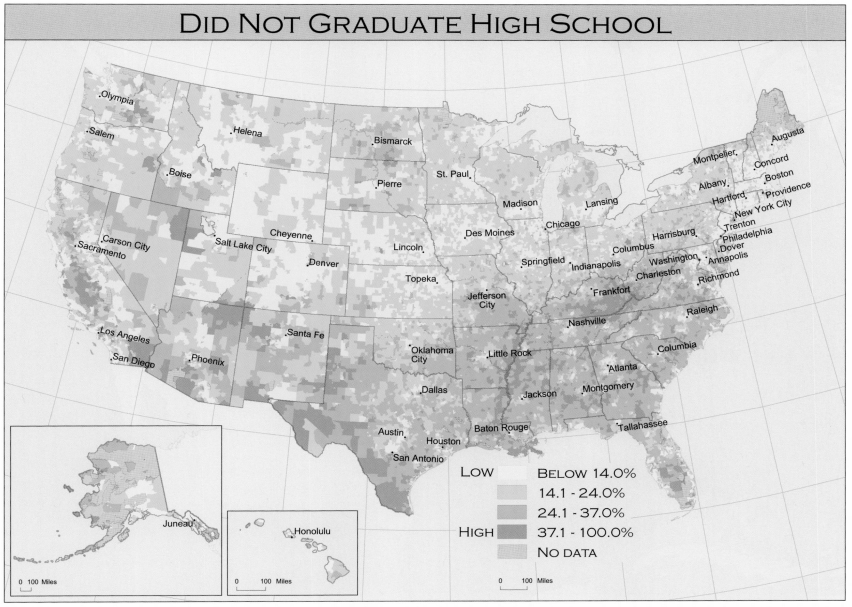

Olympia
Salem
Helena
Bismarck
Boise
St. Paul
Pierre
Madison
Lansing
Cheyenne
Des Moines
Chicago
Carson City
Salt Lake City
Lincoln
Sacramento
Denver
Springfield
Indianapolis
Columbus
Harrisburg
Montpelier
Concord
Boston
Albany
Hartford
Providence
New York City
Trenton
Philadelphia
Dover
Washington
Annapolis
Charleston
Richmond
Topeka
Jefferson City
Frankfort
Raleigh
Los Angeles
Santa Fe
Nashville
San Diego
Phoenix
Oklahoma City
Little Rock
Columbia
Dallas
Atlanta
Jackson
Montgomery
Austin
Houston
Baton Rouge
Tallahassee
San Antonio

Juneau
Honolulu

LOW   BELOW 14.0%
       14.1 - 24.0%
       24.1 - 37.0%
HIGH   37.1 - 100.0%
       NO DATA

0 100 Miles
0 100 Miles
0 100 Miles

Source: Census 2000

Did Not Graduate High School

This map shows the percentage of people aged twenty-five years and older who did not graduate from high school in areas throughout the United States.

ATTENDS ADULT EDUCATION CLASSES

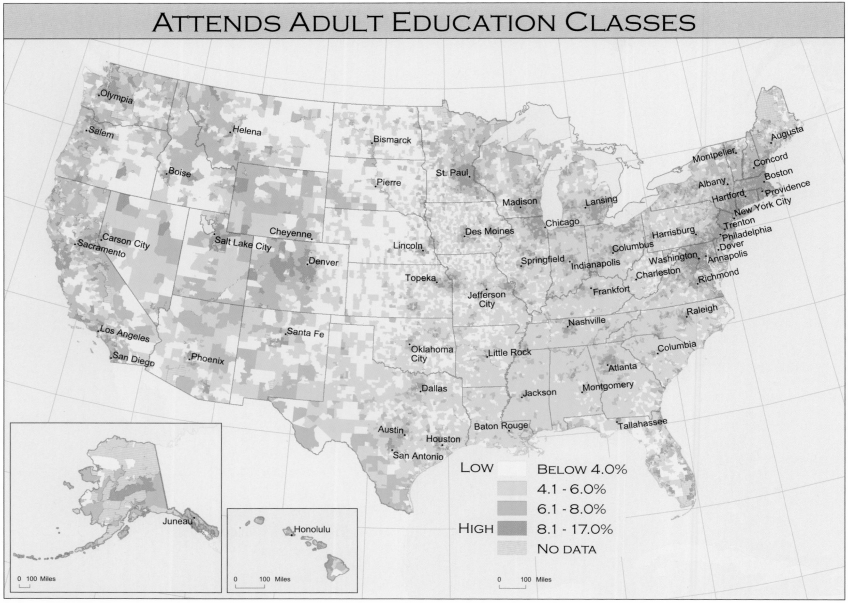

Olympia
Salem
Helena
Bismarck
Boise
Pierre
St. Paul
Madison
Lansing
Montpelier
Augusta
Concord
Albany
Boston
Hartford
Providence
New York City
Cheyenne
Carson City
Salt Lake City
Sacramento
Denver
Lincoln
Des Moines
Chicago
Harrisburg
Trenton
Columbus
Philadelphia
Dover
Springfield
Indianapolis
Washington
Annapolis
Topeka
Charleston
Richmond
Santa Fe
Jefferson City
Frankfort
Raleigh
Los Angeles
Nashville
San Diego
Phoenix
Oklahoma City
Little Rock
Columbia
Atlanta
Dallas
Jackson
Montgomery
Austin
Baton Rouge
Tallahassee
Houston
San Antonio

Juneau

Honolulu

LOW   BELOW 4.0%
       4.1 - 6.0%
       6.1 - 8.0%
HIGH   8.1 - 17.0%
       NO DATA

0 100 Miles

0 100 Miles

0 100 Miles

Sources: ESRI, Mediamark Research Inc. Doublebase 2004

Attends Adult Education Classes

This map shows the percentages of adults in the United States who attended adult education classes over a twelve-month period.

*D*ata is even more effectively presented when it is mapped. The old adage "A picture is worth a thousand words" is certainly true in this instance. Mapped data instantly conveys an accurate message and clearly illustrates the research. This book of maps decisively proves this adage.

■ ■ ■

Information about the Library of Congress is online at
www.loc.gov.

■ ■ ■

For more information about Community Tapestry
or any ESRI software products and services, visit **www.esri.com**.